What people are saying about …

TRUTH OVER TRIBE

"If you want to be a person of conviction without turning into a total jerk, read this book. If you want to have conversations with people and continue to learn and grow, read this book. If you want to find true freedom in belonging instead of the faux, enslaving community of tribalism, read this book. If you don't want these things, then you really need to read this book! *Truth Over Tribe* is a timely gift to the church, and I hope it is read widely."

Aimee Byrd, author of *The Sexual Reformation*

"This book has given me a much better understanding of how and why our country has become so dangerously polarized and fractured. But even better, it presents simple, effective examples of what we as individuals can do to help stem the tide! What a *great* and timely reminder of the blessing that comes when we take a step back and focus on keeping first things first!"

Michael Porter Jr., NBA player

"I don't know if one good and timely book can compete against the algorithms that generate billions in profits by wrecking our society. But I'm praying that Patrick Miller and Keith Simon succeed, for the sake of our churches, for the sake of our children, for the sake of our own spiritual health. Revival looks like Christians waking up to the ways political parties and their allied media seek to co-opt and corrupt our faith."

Collin Hansen, vice president of
content and editor in chief of The Gospel
Coalition, host of *Gospelbound* podcast

"*Truth Over Tribe* takes an honest look at what we are doing and why we are doing it. In a world of tribal temptations, we must be people who are true to God's Word. We were made to belong first to God. Patrick and Keith are working to lead the way."

Kyle Idleman, bestselling author of
Not a Fan and *One at a Time*

"As a gay atheist kid who fell in love with Jesus during a raging culture war between 'the gays' and 'the Christians,' I know what it's like to live in the no man's land between two warring tribes. Now decades later, when news and social media sell moral outrage and self-righteousness as a business model, Patrick Miller and Keith Simon offer this gift to the church. It's a beautiful call to realign our tribal loyalties to Jesus, a king whose business model is founded upon his own radical grace to sinners like us."

Greg Johnson, PhD, lead pastor of
Memorial Presbyterian Church of
St. Louis, author of *Still Time to Care*

"In *Truth Over Tribe*, Patrick Miller and Keith Simon address polarization, the most important issue in American society, head on.

But beyond just diagnosing the problem, Patrick and Keith go a step further—providing biblically based advice on how to navigate being a responsible and engaged citizen in the years to come."

Ryan Burge, author of *The Nones* and *20 Myths about Religion and Politics in America*

"In a time where division and quarrels are at a fever pitch, books that nudge us toward a more loving, life-giving posture are sorely needed. This is such a book. As experienced pastors and practitioners of unifying leadership around the unchanging truth of Christ, Patrick and Keith have given us a treasure in *Truth Over Tribe*. I can't recommend this book highly enough."

Scott Sauls, senior pastor of Christ Presbyterian Church and author of several books, including *A Gentle Answer* and *Beautiful People Don't Just Happen*

"Patrick and Keith focus on critical topics that need to be discovered, debated, and understood in today's Evangelical movement. In *Truth Over Tribe*, it is wonderful to see their substantial research and hear their balanced reflection."

Mike Cosper, creator and voice of *The Rise and Fall of Mars Hill* podcast

TRUTH
OVER TRIBE

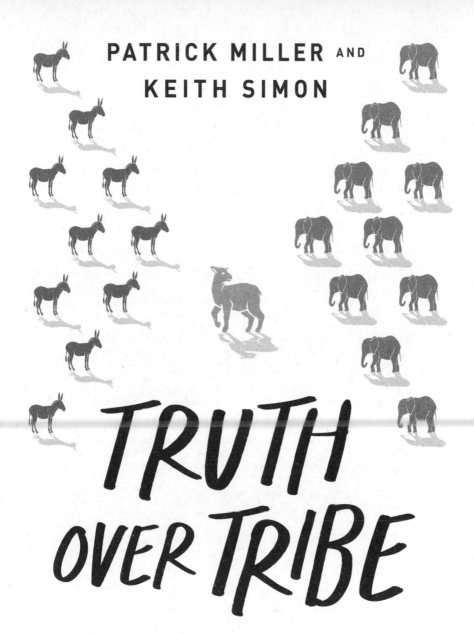

PATRICK MILLER AND KEITH SIMON

TRUTH
OVER TRIBE

PLEDGING ALLEGIANCE TO **THE LAMB,**
NOT **THE DONKEY** OR **THE ELEPHANT**

DAVID C COOK

transforming lives together

TRUTH OVER TRIBE
Published by David C Cook
4050 Lee Vance Drive
Colorado Springs, CO 80918 U.S.A.

Integrity Music Limited, a Division of David C Cook
Brighton, East Sussex BN1 2RE, England

The graphic circle C logo is a registered trademark of David C Cook.

Library of Congress Control Number 2022935639
ISBN 978-0-8307-8478-3
eISBN 978-0-8307-8479-0

The Team: Michael Covington, Michael Ross,
James Hershberger, Jack Campbell, Susan Murdock
Cover Design: Micah Kandros
Cover Photo: Shutterstock
Author Bio Photos: Kassidy Frommann

Printed in the United States of America
First Edition 2022

1 2 3 4 5 6 7 8 9 10

062022

Dedication and Acknowledgments

Truth Over Tribe is dedicated to our church, The Crossing. This book tells *our* story. You are a shining example of what happens when a community chooses truth over tribe in a culture riven by tribalism. Jesus told us not to hide our light. We did our best not to hide yours.

We want to thank our wives, Christine Simon and Emily Miller, first and foremost. You've supported us even when choosing the truth of Jesus cost you sleep, reputation, and more than a little anxiety. Without your companionship and prayers, this book—and the stories inside of it—would have crushed us.

Second, we owe a huge debt of gratitude to Anna Lynne Frazier. She helped us frame each section and read every chapter, offering feedback that made every bit of this book better.

Third, we want to thank the pastors and staff of The Crossing. Working alongside you makes the hardest days feel easy. We love being on your team.

We also want to thank Don Gates. Writing your first book is daunting, but Don's advice and encouragement made every step easier. Likewise, thank you to Michael Covington and the editorial team at David C Cook. We aren't sure why you took a risk on two unknown, first-time authors tackling a challenging topic, but we're glad you did. We hope our partnership produces good fruit in the body of Christ. Lastly, thank you to our podcast family. While we love creating content for *Ten Minute Bible Talks* and *Truth Over Tribe*, we especially *love* the community and the stories you share. Together, we can show the beauty of Jesus to a lost world.

Above all else, we want to thank Jesus. He loved us while we were his enemies, and now he calls us to do likewise.

CONTENTS

TRIBALISM IS WRECKING YOUR LIFE

I'll accept a cinnamon roll from the devil.

You don't need to be a good person, or agree with my politics, or check any identity boxes. If you offer me a cinnamon roll, I'll say thanks and enjoy every bite.

But not everyone feels the same way. For some, accepting doughy balls of sugary cinnamon goodness from the *wrong* kind of person is tantamount to compromising your integrity and makes you complicit in things you disagree with.

A Win-Win-Win

In the middle of the pandemic, when quarantining was a way of life, Love Coffee—a purveyor of delicious cinnamon rolls—was one of many local businesses in our town struggling to keep their doors open. This was especially sad because they primarily employ people with disabilities.

So The Crossing, where I am a pastor, had an idea we hoped might be a win-win-win: we'd buy a *lot* of cinnamon rolls over the course of several months so Love Coffee could stay open and the company's employees could keep their jobs. But where would we send all these cinnamon rolls? How about to people working some of the toughest jobs during the early pandemic: teachers.

Each week we sent the cinnamon rolls to different schools, giving teachers and staff a warm thank-you. Love Coffee wins. Their employees win. School staffs win.

This is the kind of thing The Crossing loves to do because we like to be known by what we're *for*, not what we're *against*. And if we break some (unfortunately well-earned) stereotypes about cantankerous Christians along the way, then even Jesus wins!

That's a four-way win. What could possibly go wrong?

How Cinnamon Rolls Got Canceled

At first, everything went smoothly. Teachers thanked us on social media, and we thanked them right back. Every week Love Coffee sent an email informing another principal that the treats were on the way.

But one week they received an unusual response. The principal turned down the cinnamon rolls. This is the email he wrote:

> I know that you all will be treating our staff due to a donation from The Crossing. I do not feel like The Crossing represents the same values we share as a staff here at _____ school. The Crossing leadership has expressed some homophobic and transphobic views and that goes against the environment that we are trying to foster here. I understand that Love Inc. and Love Coffee get a lot of support from The Crossing. I was wondering if you could bill [our school] for the treats tomorrow

and use those funds from The Crossing for something else within your organization.

The cinnamon rolls got canceled. Welcome to the era of polarization.

How Would You Respond?

What do you do when someone accuses you of the modern equivalent of leprosy? What do you do when people say you're not the kind of person they can accept a cinnamon roll from? My first thought was to say, "Okay, I'll eat *your* cinnamon rolls myself." When I realized we were sending over a hundred rolls, I needed a second thought.

Should I report this principal to the district office for misrepresenting our church and lying about our views?

Should I fire back with our own nasty email?

Should I ignore it and hope the problem didn't spread to other schools?

Should I pray the email away?

How Would Jesus Respond?

Okay, don't judge me for asking this. I swear I don't wear any weird bracelets. But *What Would Jesus Do* in this sticky situation? I think Jesus would take the principal to lunch and build a bridge—maybe even a friendship.

So that's what I did.

This wasn't the first time I'd sat across the table from someone upset at me for things that I didn't think I'd done. (No, I'm not talking about my wife. I did most of the things she's been upset with!)

The principal's email alluded to a sermon I preached in the fall of 2019, which was a tad controversial. Okay, slightly more than a tad. We were preaching through Genesis, and we came to the passage about God making humans "male and female." In my sermon, I discussed God's design for two genders and called our church to radically love our local trans community.

Maybe You Disagree with Me? That's Okay. I'd Love to Talk.

There were a wide variety of responses to that sermon, including some that were "extra." I was called Hitler and the Antichrist. I was physically threatened. We had to install security cameras at my house. Police officers patrolled our neighborhood.

Amid the vitriol, which of course lived mostly on Facebook, several people reached out personally to express sincere disagreements. I wanted to meet them to listen and learn.

So that's what I did.

I met with every person who would sit down with me.

Most of them vehemently disagreed with me on this sensitive topic, but I discovered that all of them were *good* people who cared for others. We simply differed on how to best love people struggling with gender dysphoria.

When I met with people, I started the conversation by asking them, "What do you wish I knew before I gave that sermon?" Then I wrote down everything they said in my notebook. I wasn't there to argue with them or to try to convince them I was right and they were wrong. I wanted to build a bridge. And the best way to do that was by listening and learning from other people's experiences.

I found each person to be intelligent and sincere. Hearing their stories left me with more empathy. While I did not change my perspective on the central topic, if I could do that sermon over again, I know I'd make changes to strive for even more clarity and compassion.

A New Goal for Your Next Argument

What if the goal wasn't to win an argument but to win a friend? What if we could be friends with people who hold beliefs—important beliefs—that run contrary to ours? Do those kinds of friendships make our communities better? Or do they compromise our integrity?

I think they make communities better. I think they'd make *your* life better.

So when the principal declined the cinnamon rolls, I asked him to lunch at a pizza joint. (Maybe he wasn't a dessert guy?) Conversation about our personal lives flowed easily. When we began discussing the great cinnamon-roll controversy, he told me quite a bit had changed since we originally scheduled the lunch.

> **WHAT IF THE GOAL WASN'T TO WIN AN ARGUMENT BUT TO WIN A FRIEND?**

The delay had given him more time to investigate what I publicly said on LGBTQ issues, and he realized that I didn't quite fit the angry fundamentalist stereotype.

Plus, he'd had a chance to consult some of the senior administrators in the district office. They wisely pointed out that the church wasn't asking to preach sermons to teachers. The cinnamon rolls didn't even have a "Jesus Loves You" sticker hiding anywhere.

They were just cinnamon rolls.

And the more he explained why he'd originally turned them down, the more I understood *his* perspective. He wasn't trying to make a grand political statement. He was trying to respect the opinions of one of his valued employees, who was alarmed by accepting anything from The Crossing. If I were in his situation, I might've done the same thing.

It turns out he wasn't a bad guy, and we aren't a bad church. We ended lunch by agreeing that as a culture, we've become more tribal. We have our political tribes, ideological tribes, identity tribes, and social tribes, and we're hardwired to see people outside of our groups as a hostile force for evil.

He and I agreed that we wanted to be a part of a community where people who hold to different beliefs, values, and politics can work together for the common good.

But the only way that will happen is if we build relationships, listen to one another, and are open minded enough to consider opposing views. The vast majority of the people who live in your community are sincere and share many of the same hopes and fears that you do.

Jesus didn't come to earth to recruit culture warriors. He came to recruit disciples who imitated his sacrificial love. He came to announce that through his work, God's kingdom of love, justice, and mercy was coming on earth as in heaven, and *everyone* was invited. You didn't need to be morally pure to join him. You didn't need a certain set of politics to qualify. You didn't need a certain racial or sexual identity to be welcomed. The only requirement was to follow him.

Our culture desperately needs students of Jesus, schooled in the ways of enemy love, humility, meekness, *and* truth-telling. Jesus offers the ultimate solution to the tribalism that is tearing our community apart: transforming humans, with all their tribal tendencies, from the inside out.

Your life will be more rich, full, generous, and loving if you become a student of his way. This book is a small step in that direction. You'll learn how tribalism makes your life miserable (part 1), why tribalism animates our cultural moment (part 2), and how Jesus offers you a path out of tribalism (part 3).

I hope this book brings healing in your family, friendships, and community by giving you a taste of heaven's love on earth.

One final note: you probably noticed this book has two authors. We chose not to announce the specific author behind every story because this book isn't about us (and trust us, it would get annoying). If curiosity is killing you, hit one of us up on Twitter: @PatrickKMiller_ or @KeithSimon_. We'll respond.

Discussion and Reflection Questions

1. Imagine that a group sent you cinnamon rolls as a thank-you for your hard work. Is there any group whose offer you would refuse? Why?

2. Make a list of *good* traits of individuals within that group.

3. How can you pray for the members of that group?

Part One

How Tribalism Hurts You

Do you feel tension in relationships that once upon a time felt close and peaceful?

If so, you're not alone. In this section, we look at five ways tribalism is hurting you. And if you're being honest, you'll find more than a few ways that your own tribalism might be hurting others. The only way to solve a problem is to name it, mourn it, and turn from it.

You'll learn how tribalism is hurting your closest relationships (chapter 1), escalating your anxiety (chapter 2), incentivizing inauthenticity (chapter 3), making unnecessary enemies (chapter 4), and blinding you to what's true (chapter 5).

As you read these chapters, our prayer is that Jesus will give you eyes to see your own tribalism and set you free. If you're a fan of self-reflection, scan the QR code below and take our "How Tribal Are You?" quiz.

Chapter 1

Tribalism Ruins Your Relationships

Reunions have never been my thing. If I wanted to stay in touch with you, I would have. If I haven't talked to you in a decade, there's probably a reason.

In fact, I'd rather have a colonoscopy than attend a high school reunion. (Pro tip: Colonoscopies are pretty amazing. A cleanse followed by a dose of propofol. Woke up like a champ. Best sleep I've ever had.)

But family reunions are almost inescapable. My friend Susan is a saint who attends them without complaint. She went to her new husband's family reunion in a park on a day in which the temperature and humidity were competing for top honors. Going to your in-laws' reunion is not nearly as bad as your own. When you're on foreign territory, you can always point at the crazies and say to your spouse, "If our kids end up like *that*, we will know whose genes they got."

During the reunion, somewhere between the potato salad and softball, someone proudly proclaimed that she'd never vote for Trump. She was Never Trump to her core. Nearby was a Trump supporter who had had enough Busch Lights that he didn't hold his tongue. Words were exchanged. The mood turned sour. Not so long ago that would've been the end of it. By the time the next reunion rolled around, everyone would have forgotten, or at least pretended to.

But thank goodness for Facebook. It's the perfect place for family disagreements to go nuclear.

After a few heated FB exchanges, the Never Trumpers decided to boycott the funeral of a family member—the father of young children who'd died suddenly of an aggressive form of brain cancer. They'd rather miss the funeral than see their pro-Trump relatives.

Their absence was painful and *noticed*.

The Trumpers responded with wedding disinvitations. And on it went. Years later, they still haven't reconciled.

Tribalism Is Destroying Families

You know the story. Tribalism is tearing families, friend groups, communities, and churches apart. It's making your life miserable and lonely.

One reason for the increased anxiety is social isolation caused by political polarization.

Walking away from longtime friendships because the person's politics are different from yours comes with a hefty price tag. *All Things Considered* reported that Los Angeles resident Shama Davis, a consultant, told a friend of twenty-five years to "lose my number" because he thought the friend was downplaying police brutality. "I don't respect you now. I don't. Because people are really dying."

Joni Jensen of New York outdid him by ending a forty-year relationship over the Brett Kavanaugh hearings. She told NPR, "I just hung up on my end and proceeded to just block him in every possible way."[1]

Have you lost a friend or family member because of polarization? Do your relationships feel more tense? Are you tired of walking on eggshells around someone you once trusted?

Somehow, the ideologues of the day convinced you and your friends that your political tribe is more important than your family and friends. They got you to believe that the world will be better and you will be happier if you adamantly defend your tribe's perspective—even at the expense of deep relationships. Or that if you listen to someone who disagrees with you and assume the best, you're a "cheese-eating surrender monkey."[2]

But is this the path to happiness or misery?

Would You Rather?

You know those dumb icebreaker questions you get asked when joining a group for the first time? Would you rather live by the beach or the mountains?

My wife and I have learned that the right answer to that question is "friends." Wouldn't you rather dig ditches in the desert with friends than live in your version of paradise by yourself?

In 1938, with the hope of discovering what leads to happiness, researchers began following two groups: Harvard students and boys from Boston's poorest neighborhoods. (All the students were male because Harvard didn't fully accept women as students until 1977.) Now, more than eighty years later, only a few of the original subjects are still alive.

Interestingly, two of the participants were President John F. Kennedy and Ben Bradlee, the longtime and influential editor of the *Washington Post*. Over the decades, the researchers expanded the study to include the family members of the original subjects and others in the original neighborhoods.

Here's what the *Harvard Gazette* concluded: "Close relationships, more than money or fame, are what keep people happy throughout their lives." Those relationships "are better predictors of long and happy lives than social class, IQ, or even genes."[3]

Or you could have just read Genesis 2:18: "The LORD God said, 'It is not good for the man to be alone.'"

You see the problem, I'm sure. Our happiness and life satisfaction depend on the very relationships that tribalism is ending. So who suffers? You suffer.

Why Don't We Stop Talking Politics?

Friends have told me that the best way to keep personal or work friendships is to stay quiet about your political opinions. That's the strategy journalist Judith Margolis Friedman found effective for so long. She kept her political views to herself because she knew that to express them was to risk "not only social suicide but potentially career-ending and family-ties-rendering."[4]

While it can be wise to avoid certain topics with certain groups at certain times, that shouldn't be the way we live all the time.

Maybe it's just me, but I can handle only so much talk about kids' sports before I want to ram a salad fork into my eye. My tolerance for spicy conversations is higher than my tolerance for spicy foods. I love a dinner conversation with a friend who has a different perspective than me and who can intelligently talk through it. It's not about trying to change each other's minds as much as it is seeing an issue from a different perspective.

I hope you're confident enough in what you believe to handle having your beliefs challenged and open minded enough to change your mind if warranted. If nothing else, having friends with diverse beliefs makes life more interesting.

I HOPE YOU'RE CONFIDENT ENOUGH IN WHAT YOU BELIEVE TO HANDLE HAVING YOUR BELIEFS CHALLENGED AND OPEN MINDED ENOUGH TO CHANGE YOUR MIND IF WARRANTED.

What We Learn from George Bush and Ellen DeGeneres

You can do this. I know you can because Ellen DeGeneres and George Bush did it and they have more to lose than you and I do.

When the talk show host and former president sat next to each other in Jerry Jones's suite at a Dallas Cowboys game, a picture of them went viral, and the haters did what they always do—hate.

The following week on her show, Ellen addressed the response to the picture. "During the game, they showed a shot of me and George laughing together. And so, people were upset. They thought, *Why is a gay Hollywood liberal sitting next to a conservative Republican president?*

"Here's the thing," she added. "I'm friends with George Bush. In fact, I'm friends with a lot of people who don't share the same beliefs that I have. We're all different and I think that we've forgotten that that's okay."

DeGeneres continued: "When I say, 'Be kind to one another,' I don't mean only the people that think the same way that you do. I mean be kind to everyone. Doesn't matter."[5]

I think Jesus would give Ellen and George a standing ovation.

Why? Because Jesus brought together the most economically, racially, geographically diverse set of followers in the history of the world. He taught them that they could be in relationship with one another despite their differences. He taught them that as significant as their differences were, those differences paled in comparison with what they shared in common.

This is really your choice. Do you want to isolate yourself or be in community? Do you want to limit conversations to the safe subjects, or do you want to explore more interesting and spicy topics? Do you want to surround yourself with people who think just like you do, or do you want to learn and be challenged? Do you want painful, pride-wrecked relationships with family and friends? Or do you want love powerful enough to outlast conflict created by names on a ballot?

> DO YOU WANT PAINFUL, PRIDE-WRECKED
> RELATIONSHIPS WITH FAMILY AND FRIENDS? OR DO
> YOU WANT LOVE POWERFUL ENOUGH TO OUTLAST
> CONFLICT CREATED BY NAMES ON A BALLOT?

Here's the key to relationships that can't be broken by tribalism. Share a love that's rooted in something stronger and more everlasting than today's tribal boundaries: Jesus. His followers don't have the same politics, wealth, race, and gender, but they all call him Lord.

Discussion and Reflection Questions

1. Which relationships in your life have been negatively impacted by tribalism?

2. How have you contributed to the hurt?

3. How is God calling you to bring healing to those relationships?

Chapter 2

TRIBALISM MAKES YOU ANXIOUS

On April 27, 2021, *Jeopardy!* contestant Kelly Donohue made a hand gesture, which you might think represented the number three. But an elite Facebook group of former contestants saw it for what they were certain it was: a covert white supremacist hand signal.[1]

The once-docile kings and queens of nerdom were outraged. *How could the producers miss this? How could they allow Donohue to besmirch the legacy of their beloved franchise?* Many members took to scouring Donohue's social media, where they found other alarming signs of white supremacy: he supported Donald Trump and once posted a picture of Frank Sinatra. One group member noted his use of "gypsy" during an answer on the show.

Donohue was in the *other* tribe; therefore, he was a wolf.

Donohue, for his part, tried to explain that he was holding up a three for his third victory. He also condemned white supremacy. But rather than absolving himself, he only proved to the contestant community that he was a *covert* white supremacist operative. A wolf in sheep's clothing.

Members of the Facebook group wrote a letter explaining the travesty to the Anti-Defamation League (ADL), which is normally

quick to file lawsuits if there's even the smallest hint of white
supremacy.

After a few days, the ADL sent the Facebook group the following email:

> Thank you for reaching out regarding your con-
> cern over a Jeopardy [sic] contestant flashing what
> you believed to be a white power hand signal. We
> have reviewed the tape and it looks like he is sim-
> ply holding up three fingers when they say he is a
> three-time champion.[2]

The ADL noted that while it's true that a small group of white
supremacists tried to co-opt the "OK" hand signal (which looks
like a three), Donohue wasn't even using that gesture. He was simply holding up a rather awkward-looking number three.

The website Snopes agreed. It published photos of Donohue at
the end of every game he'd won. After his first win, he held up the
number one. After his second win, two. After his third win, *three*.

Unfortunately, Donohue's fellow contestants could not be con-
vinced. He was a *wolf*. One wrote, "We saw it. We know we did.
But a lot of people (including the goddamned Anti-Defamation
League) are telling us we didn't. That's some classic gaslighting."[3]

Many bystanders wanted to speak up for Donohue at this
point. *Clearly* the former contestants had misunderstood the situation. But no one did speak up. Why place yourself in the cross
fire? Why risk losing your place in the community? Why risk your
own reputation?

As for Donohue, he's been harassed on social media ever since, and his personal reputation is a wreck.

Three Forms of Anxiety

How you react to this story says a lot about you.

Do you empathize with the community? Do you fear that we're too slow to condemn bad behavior, thus making our world less safe for the marginalized?

Do you empathize with Kelly Donohue? Do you fear that something like that could happen to you if you send the wrong email, say the wrong word, or make (however innocently) the wrong hand gesture?

Do you empathize with the bystanders? Do you fear speaking out when people unfairly malign others in your own community because you know they might turn on you next?

Tribalism cranks up everyone's anxiety, although it looks different from person to person.

- **The Anxiety of the Crusaders:** Crusaders fear those outside their tribe. They see the other tribe's ideas as *dangerous* for society. They anxiously worry that if no one speaks or acts, people *will be hurt*. Thus, they take up the crusader's mantle for justice and truth. They hunt down even the faintest hint of unrighteousness. Membership in a different tribe—be it supporting Trump or supporting critical race theory—is evidence of extreme culpability. Their fear makes it difficult to hear nuance or change direction once a crusade is started.

- **The Anxiety of the Hunted:** The hunted fear being canceled. They live in a soup of low-level anxiety, fearing that one misinterpreted word, one uncharitably read email, one innocent hand gesture might trip a land mine they couldn't see. As a result, they're hesitant to share their opinions, especially about anything controversial. They constantly size up others to determine, "Are you in my tribe? Can I be honest with you?" Their guarded existence makes them feel increasingly embattled, even if no one's actively trying to wreck their reputation.

- **The Anxiety of the Bystanders:** Bystanders fear breaking with their own tribe to speak truth. To bystanders, the crusades of crusaders are obviously unfair, but they avoid speaking out. They know that doing so places them in the crusader's crosshairs and may lead their tribe to disown them. Thus, they carefully monitor their own speech. On the one hand, they don't want to condone the crusades, but on the other hand, they don't want to appear like sympathizers.

In a tribalized society, no one escapes the anxiety. You might find yourself experiencing one form one day and a different form the next.

The Anxiety of the Crusaders

Olivia, a Latina student at Claremont McKenna College (CMC), wrote a public essay sharing the pain she experienced when she discovered that people who looked like her were better represented among blue-collar staff (janitors, facility managers, landscapers) than white-collar staff (administrators, professors, deans).

The dean of students, Mary Spellman, responded to her privately: "Thank you for writing and sharing this article with me. We have a lot to do as a college and community. Would you be willing to talk with me sometime about these issues? They are important to me and the staff and we are working on how we can better serve students, especially those who don't fit our CMC mold. I would love to talk with you more."[4]

The response seems sincere. But three words stick out: *our CMC mold.*

Negatively, they could be taken to imply that the student's ethnicity made her a *misfit.* Charitably, they could be read as a faltering attempt to affirm Olivia's experience: she feels like an outsider who breaks the mold, and Spellman wants to change that.

In a non-anxious society, one can easily imagine Spellman's response opening a fruitful dialogue in which both parties assume the best, help each other grow, and improve their shared institution. But a crusader's anxiety makes it almost impossible for her to listen to others charitably. Small offenses cause tremendous mental pain. The crusader suddenly feels like a victim. The offender is transmuted into a monster, an unrighteous threat to society, which easily justifies a muscular, crusading, antagonistic reaction.

The crusader's anxiety triumphed at CMC. Fear about harmful speech justified protests, hunger strikes, and ultimately Spellman's resignation.

I sincerely wonder whether, with years of retrospect, any of the students who participated feel regret. Do they feel guilty about ending Spellman's career? Do they see they missed an opportunity for constructive dialogue that could've led to lasting change? Or do they still view the world as a black-and-white battle between good and evil, configuring themselves as the righteous oppressed and their enemies—be it "the demonic left" or "the white supremacist right"—as the unrighteous infidels?

If you identify with the crusaders, ask yourself these questions: Does living in constant fear of the other tribe make your life richer? What if your tribalism is manufacturing unnecessary anxiety in your life?

The Anxiety of the Hunted

When I was six years old, a *massive* dog chased me down the street from a neighbor's yard. I can still see its wolfish canines bared, chomping, chasing, ready to take me down and attack me. As I ran, I looked desperately for a stick or a shovel or something to defend myself but found nothing. So I just screamed. I yelled as loud as I could in complete and utter terror.

Thankfully my mom heard. She came outside, rescued me ... and then she pet the dog.

To this day, I'm not sure whether the dog was *actually* massive. I'm not even sure that it was chasing me down for dinner. It now seems quite likely that it was a Pomeranian enjoying a fun game of chase with a little boy who was delightedly screaming, "Mommy!"

What I *can* say is that I've never felt more fear in my entire life. That's silly to admit because I've been in far more dangerous situations. But the truth is that fear and anxiety are not always proportional to actual risk.

Perhaps more importantly, fear and anxiety are helpful in *actual* life-threatening situations. If that dog wanted to eat me, searching for a weapon as I ran away screaming was the smartest thing possible. But fear and anxiety are a disservice when you aren't at risk. They cause you to see threats where none exist.

FEAR AND ANXIETY ARE NOT ALWAYS PROPORTIONAL TO ACTUAL RISK.

This describes the mental labyrinth experienced by those suffering from the anxiety of the hunted. You hear stories like the one above and increasingly find it difficult to tell the difference between Pomeranians and wolves. You begin to wonder which encounter, conversation, email, Facebook post, or text message might cost you your job and reputation. So you tiptoe through mazelike conversations to suss out someone's politics, causes, triggers.

The biggest problem with feeling hunted is that you *rarely* stay in this form of anxiety. Either you exit by creating painful distance between yourself and others, or you transition into a silent crusader. Behind closed doors and on private threads you rail against the wolves lurking in the shadows. Your fear increases, whether or not anyone is *actually* out to get you, and it gives you a near-pathological certainty that everyone in the *other* tribe is a wolf.

Ironically, the more you fear the *other*, the more wolfish you will become. If you think a wolf has you cornered, not only will you experience an unpleasant sense of helplessness; you will justify snapping and biting to escape.

Suddenly, Jesus's commands to love your neighbor, live with meekness, walk in humility, bless your enemy, and turn the other cheek sound hopelessly naive. You justify disobeying him because you think your personal context is so extraordinarily dangerous that ordinary Christian ethics no longer apply.

If you feel the anxiety of the hunted, ask yourself this question: Is anyone actively trying to harm your reputation in a significant way or attempting to get you fired for your beliefs?

If the answer is yes, then your fear is a healthy response. Seek help. But don't become a crusader. If the answer is no—and in most cases the answer is no—then realize that people from the other tribe are not trying to harm you. They simply disagree. You aren't in their crosshairs.

In the end, remind yourself that no one can steal your reputation before Jesus. No one can steal your eternal life with him. No hunter alive can take what you long to hear: Jesus telling you, "Well done, good and faithful servant."[5]

The Anxiety of the Bystanders

What should you do when you see your tribe embarking on an unholy crusade? Perhaps you feel anxious. *I can't participate in this. But if I resist, what will happen to me?*

David French is a well-known author and attorney who spent his early career with conservative law organizations fighting for religious liberty and advocating for conservative policies. But he found Donald Trump's rhetoric around race and "shithole" countries alarming, not least because he and his wife adopted their daughter from Ethiopia.[6]

This led him to speak out against Trump as a candidate and as president. French never stopped being a conservative, but as a reward for critiquing the leader of his tribe, he was publicly maligned by former colleagues as a "coward" who was trying to "court favor with elites."[7]

Anonymous trolls photoshopped his daughter's picture into gas chambers and slave fields. They hacked into his phone calls to yell profanities. They texted him racial slurs and left voice mails of people screaming. The FBI told him in 2018 that a known bomber and Trump superfan was googling his address. People sent photos of murders and suicides to his wife. She lost job opportunities. Men confronted her at her child's Christian school to condemn her.

This is *exactly* what all bystanders fear. If you speak a word against your tribe, you will not open fruitful dialogue. You'll become a target. The crusaders in your own tribe will do everything they can to make you miserable. Their message is clear: repent or disappear.

The cost of allowing your bystander anxiety to silence you is simple: you lose your integrity. Some would rather live as cowards than die with bravery. I get it. But Christians should not be those people.

Micah 6:8 simply calls you "to do justice, and to love kindness, and to walk humbly with your God" (ESV). You can do this because you know that *nothing*—even abandonment by your tribe—can separate you from the love of God.

In the Company of the Prophets

In the centuries following Israel's civil war in 913 BC, the northern kingdom of Israel descended into a hopeless pattern of idolatry. Yahweh became a god in the pantheon of Canaanite deities. Under the rule of Ahab and Jezebel, idolatry reached its apex. They removed Yahweh from the pantheon and declared Ba'al, the god of fertility, king over all other gods. With idolatry came terrible acts of injustice and temple prostitution. Ahab used his monarchical power to oppress, steal, and murder with impunity.

To stand up against Ahab's regime and Jezebel's god was to ask for a death sentence. The Ba'al priests were on a crusade to root out any Yahweh worship—fearing that Yahwistic resistance might threaten their own priestly authority.

Those who remembered Yahweh felt hunted. And in a real sense this was *legitimate* fear. In the court, there were also bystanders who knew the wrongness of it all but said nothing.

All except Elijah.

> NOTHING—EVEN ABANDONMENT
> BY YOUR TRIBE—CAN SEPARATE
> YOU FROM THE LOVE OF GOD.

In 1 Kings 18, Elijah had a showdown with Ba'al prophets on Mount Carmel. He showed—with a miraculous fireworks display that would put the best Fourth of July parties to shame—that Yahweh was *real* and Ba'al was *imaginary*.

The crowds ran the Ba'al priests out of town, and it seemed as if Elijah had won a decisive victory. But it was short lived. We pick up the story in 1 Kings 19:1–2:

> Now Ahab told Jezebel everything Elijah had done and how he had killed all the prophets with the sword. So Jezebel sent a messenger to Elijah to say, "May the gods deal with me, be it ever so severely, if by this time tomorrow I do not make your life like that of one of them."

Elijah was a hunted fugitive. The anxiety of that (very real) hunt sent him into a monthlong depressive state. He hardly ate. He hardly spoke. He slept all day. And finally, he had three encounters with Yahweh at the top of Mount Sinai, where he claimed to be the last Yahweh worshipper alive.

His words recall Moses's words on top of Sinai, after Israel worshipped the golden calf. At that time, Yahweh offered to destroy the whole nation and start over with Moses. But Moses refused. He interceded for forgiveness.

Elijah, it seemed, wanted God to give him the same offer. An offer that he, unlike Moses, intended to accept. He went from being the hunted one to a violent crusader in a short period of time.

Yahweh never gave him that offer, though. Instead, he told Elijah that he was out of touch with reality. Many people still worshipped

Yahweh and had not bowed down before Ba'al. Yes, Elijah was hunted at that moment, but that was *not* the end of the story. Yahweh had plans to deal with the problem of Ahab and Jezebel that extended far beyond Elijah.

But if Elijah wanted to participate, he could not be a bystander. He could not give in to the anxiety of being hunted. He could not become a crusader. No, he simply needed to trust that Yahweh had things under control.

Jesus has things under control in your life. In your family. In your city. In your nation. *That* is reality. Don't let the unrealities of tribalism steal that peace.

Discussion and Reflection Questions

1. Which forms of anxiety does tribalism cause you to experience (anxiety of the crusader, the hunted, or the bystander)? What do you fear losing as a result of tribalism in our culture?

2. How does your tribalism cause anxiety in the lives of others?

3. How is God calling you to trust him with your specific form of anxiety?

Chapter 3

Tribalism Incentivizes Inauthenticity

American culture today is marked by a refreshing trend toward authenticity that includes a refusal to conform to other people's expectations. Pastors now gain followers by authentically sharing their struggles instead of pretending to have it all together. More people expect companies to not only produce good products but also do good works. In the name of authenticity people are pushing back against curated, photoshopped social media feeds. All this stems from the belief that authenticity leads to a happier life.

This is supported by Bronnie Ware's experience with patients as a hospice nurse. In her book *The Top Five Regrets of the Dying*, she wrote that the number one regret she encountered was living an inauthentic life—"I wish I'd had the courage to live a life true to myself, not the life others expected of me."[1]

But there's another kind of authenticity that we're less sure of, more suspicious of, less enthusiastic about: intellectual authenticity.

Intellectual authenticity is the willingness to publicly hold and state beliefs that don't conform to the expectations of the prevailing tribe. Often, a high price is exacted from those who are honest about their thoughts, opinions, and beliefs.

Dorian Abbot, an associate professor in the geophysical sciences at the University of Chicago, faced a temptation to do what others expected of him, but he chose courage instead. In the fall of 2021, he was disinvited from giving a prestigious lecture at MIT because of his honestly held beliefs. His crime? Advocating for merit-based evaluations in higher education. Rather than changing his perspective to appease the crowd, Abbot stood his ground.[2]

He was committed to intellectual authenticity.

Why didn't Dorian Abbot change his position to conform to those in power? Sure, it wouldn't have been authentic. But if he had changed it, he could've ended the criticism, bolstered his professional reputation, and garnered more speaking opportunities.

A little inauthenticity can go a long way.

But do we want to live in a world that incentivizes inauthenticity? Do we want to live in a world where "speaking out would likely bring serious reputational and professional consequences"?[3]

Or consider J. K. Rowling, who received tremendous criticism online for stating that she believes that biological sex is real. Rowling refused to acquiesce to those who demand that we perform linguistic gymnastics to avoid using the word *woman* when discussing pregnancy and female reproductive health. Despite the continued controversy, she's still standing her ground.[4]

Set aside whether you agree with her. Doesn't authenticity demand honesty on her part?

Both Rowling and Abbot faced vitriolic critiques for their intellectual authenticity. People in the opposing tribes have called for resignations and boycotts. Both stand to gain a great deal by changing their public positions. If they did, the tribes that rail against them might welcome them back in.

We all face difficult questions that demand uncomfortable answers. Will you be authentic even when it comes with a cost? Do you value intellectual authenticity for everyone or only for those you agree with, who are part of your tribe?

WILL YOU BE AUTHENTIC EVEN WHEN IT COMES WITH A COST?

Most of us aren't as courageous as Rowling or Abbot. And it's because tribalism has incentivized inauthenticity.

System Failure or a Dishonest System?

In grad school, I learned that a system can promote dishonesty.

Inside the Master of Divinity track, 99 percent of the seminary's resources were invested in preparing future pastors academically and theologically. Field education was the 1 percent designed to give students practical ministry experience.

I had spent the past nine years in campus ministry, so I was far more interested in the academics than field ed. I didn't expect to learn much from an overworked pastor who knew I wasn't going to be around long term. But I get that a seminary's sales pitch to prospective students can't be: "You'll graduate with a lot of knowledge *and* an inability to talk to real people!"

Despite what I saw as a waste of time, I played the game and "did" my field ed.

Unfortunately, the field ed requirements were so onerous that even a well-intentioned student and mentor could never achieve them. Pastors and students filled out forms claiming they met with a frequency that defied reality. Pastors signed off on projects that were impossible to complete. Everyone knew it was a game.

Looking back on it, what I did—playing the game and signing the forms—was wrong. I wish I would have done the right thing to get the most out of that part of my education, even if it meant working to change the system.

The real cost of field education wasn't my time. *It was my integrity.* And the integrity of the mentors I served.

Sometimes good intentions create systems that foster dishonesty.

And the same thing can happen with authenticity. Today's political tribalism—however well-intended its advocates may be—is creating a system that cultivates inauthenticity.

Tribalism Encourages Dishonesty

Tribes value loyalty. That's why they impose social costs on group members who break with the tribe's orthodoxy.

Of course, some people think these costs are just. Others hope the costs will cause people to reconsider their beliefs and change their minds. But punishing people who share information and speak their minds only incentivizes silence and intellectual inauthenticity.

Carefully listening to opposing views, being open to new information, a willingness to change one's mind, nuance, compromise—the very things that promote social cohesion and intellectual progress—are seen as threats by tribalism.

Take this example: In October 2021, the University of Florida barred three of its political science professors from testifying in a voting rights lawsuit against the administration of Governor Ron

DeSantis. This reversed the university's previous policy about offering public testimony.[5] Do you think silencing these professors changed their minds? Do you think it was just or fair? Of course not. But I guarantee the professors and others at the university got the message: intellectual authenticity will not be tolerated here.

The only way to incentivize intellectual authenticity is to encourage a free and open debate. That's exactly what *Harper's Magazine* was trying to do when it published an article titled "A Letter on Justice and Open Debate" in the summer of 2020. The 152 signatories, most of whom find themselves politically on the center-left, called for an end to the practice of exacting reputational costs on those entering public debate in good faith.

The letter reads in part: "This stifling atmosphere will ultimately harm the most vital causes of our time. The restriction of debate, whether by a repressive government or an intolerant society, invariably hurts those who lack power and makes everyone less capable of democratic participation. The way to defeat bad ideas is by exposure, argument, and persuasion, not by trying to silence or wish them away."[6]

They nailed it. You change minds through persuasion and debate, not enforcing the loyalty oaths of tribalism.

Unfortunately, people rarely embrace this form of authenticity. Even in the church.

When the Church Punished Intellectual Authenticity

Galileo was a brilliant Italian professor known for being a bit of a contrarian when it came to conventional wisdom. He didn't leave his mark by inventing the telescope but by turning it toward the heavens. What he saw lay in direct opposition to the long-held Aristotelian view that Earth was the center of the universe, instead confirming Copernicus's contrasting hypothesis.

This discovery put Galileo at odds with the official dogma of the Catholic Church, which was rooted in the belief that everything revolved around the earth. Galileo never intended to disrupt faith. He didn't believe his discoveries contradicted the Bible, only that the Bible had been misread.

In 1616, the powers that be within the Catholic Church forbade Galileo from teaching or defending the Copernican theory. He complied for seven years. Then in 1623, a new pope was elected who had a personal friendship with Galileo and gave him some leeway in publishing his work. But it didn't take long for Galileo to push things further than his friend the pope was comfortable with. In 1633, Galileo was tried for the heresy of teaching that the sun was the center of the universe. Interrogated under the threat of torture, Galileo was found guilty and sentenced to house arrest for the rest of his life.[7]

Learning from Past Mistakes

To fairly consider how church leaders ended up in this position, we will need to put ourselves in their seventeenth-century shoes.

For centuries, theologians and biblical scholars have affirmed that the Bible says the earth is the center of the universe. Suddenly, an arrogant professor arrives claiming he knows more than the Bible and what our naked eyes reveal every day.

What do we do?

Is the only option to declare Galileo wrong and forbid him from teaching or sharing his belief?

Obviously not. Why not allow Galileo to share his beliefs without fear of consequences? If he's right, then we'll all learn something. If he's wrong, then that will become obvious before the idea does much damage.

But whatever we do, let's not set up a system that suppresses the truth. Why? Because when you keep people from sharing their beliefs, it's inevitable that we'll all get dumber and continue to believe the modern equivalent of the sun rotating around the earth.

More importantly, the knife cuts both ways. Do you want the freedom to be intellectually authentic without social cost? Of course you do. So apply the golden rule and do unto others as you want them to do to you: build a system that ensures the freedom to be authentic.

Should We Tell Him He's Naked?

The Emperor's New Clothes is a children's story by Hans Christian Andersen about a proud, fashion-loving ruler.

Enter two swindlers who come to town promising the emperor that, for the right price, they can weave the most beautiful clothes. These clothes will have the added benefit of being invisible to fools. Not only will the emperor be well dressed, but with these clothes, he'll be able to distinguish the wise from the foolish.[8]

Neither the emperor nor his officials can see the clothes, but no one dares admit it, because no one wants to be exposed as a fool, unworthy of their job.

The emperor buys the clothes, puts them on, and parades naked through the streets while everyone admires, in very specific detail, how much they love his outfit. And all this because no one dares to state an opinion that runs contrary to perceived wisdom.

Until a child speaks out.

A young boy says what everyone else knows, even if they won't admit it. "He hasn't got anything on!" After that, the whole town is willing to say the quiet part out loud.

The emperor was a fool not because he couldn't see the "clothes" but because he'd disincentivized people to tell the truth. It shouldn't surprise us that *only* a young child was naive enough to tell the truth in a room that didn't want to hear it. The older we get, the more aware we are of the social pressures to conform to the tribe. Intellectual authenticity takes courage because we know the potential consequences.

Can you be as courageous as a child?

What Courage Is and Isn't

We want to live in a culture that incentivizes authenticity. This means encouraging free and open debate. But that culture will only exist if we're willing to courageously speak truth and stand up for others' rights to do the same. We must resist the urge to pile on, destroy people's reputations, and take away their livelihoods in response to intellectual authenticity that threatens our positions.

Today, few people are willing to courageously pursue intellectual authenticity. Sure, lots of people put on the act. But it's not courageous ...

… to proclaim things that your tribe agrees with.

… to allow your tribe to determine your beliefs.

… to criticize the other tribe.

Courage is doing the right thing, the intellectually authentic thing, despite the costs. And only your tribe—those you respect—can impose costs. If the other side disagrees with you, that might even raise your standing within your own tribe (just look at how some conservatives brag that CNN hates them, and vice versa). If your tribe is constantly praising you, that's a good indication you haven't done anything particularly courageous. You do not have to be brave to fit in. If you want to identify someone with *real* intellectual authenticity, look for acts of intellectual courage. It is courageous …

… to publicly disagree with your tribe.

… to hold to your honestly held beliefs in a tribe that demands intellectual conformity.

… to publicly agree with an opposing tribe.

If you're afraid of the costs imposed on you by your tribe, you'll be unwilling to say what you believe. This is what inauthenticity looks like. You're going to nod along with the group even when your conscience is bothered. You're going to laugh when your heart says to protest. You're going to become a dishonest person afraid to say what you really think.

God Loves Intellectual Authenticity

An underappreciated aspect of the biblical story is that God never coerces belief. Instead, he allows humans to freely choose to follow him.

Perhaps this doesn't sound radical in our democratic age, but in the ancient world, this kind of freedom of thought was unheard of. For example, Babylon enrolled prisoners of war in the state's Leadership Academy. Unlike today's universities, this school didn't allow students to design their own majors. Everyone learned "the language and literature of the Babylonians." And it didn't stop there.

In Babylon, citizens and foreigners alike were compelled to worship the divine image of the king under threat of death. Persia, which replaced Babylon, was slightly more tolerant, but Daniel still ended up in the lions' den for praying to the wrong god. And then there's Rome, which invented crucifixion to intimidate potential opponents into silence.

GOD NEVER COERCES BELIEF.

In contrast stands Jesus, who rejected violence and never threatened or argued anyone into the kingdom of God. He offered the rich young ruler a choice. He invited his disciples to follow him and then allowed them to challenge him and even leave him. Perhaps it's no surprise that he told people they must become like little children—honest, truth-telling children—to enter his kingdom. "The way, the truth, and the life" isn't threatened by disagreement and doesn't encourage intellectual inauthenticity.

Discussion and Reflection Questions

1. How is your fear of your own tribe leading you to be inauthentic about your true beliefs and thoughts? How is your fear of the other tribe leading you in that same inauthentic way?

2. In what ways has your own tribalism led people around you to be inauthentic about their ideas and beliefs?

3. What steps is God calling you to take in order to live authentically for his glory? What truth do you need to courageously speak to your own tribe?

Chapter 4

Tribalism Creates Your Enemies

"Are you really sure they're *all* bad people?" I asked.

He responded with a confidence few can muster: "*They* are out to get us. *They* want to see us fail. *They* will deploy any policy *they* can imagine to put us behind."

He wasn't talking about his business rivals, or his wife's best friends. He was talking about *the left*. Apparently, Joe Biden, Nancy Pelosi, and Chuck Schumer are in a massive conspiracy with evil media elites to destroy people like him—everyday white guys.

I pointed out that he lived in a nice house, had a healthy family, and ran a successful business. Surely they weren't out to destroy those things? And if they were, they didn't seem to be very good at it. I granted that a small number of people might want to hurt all white men. But I had a hard time believing this was the animating motivation behind *all* liberal politicians and voters.

He demurred. I was just choosing not to see reality.

Fast-forward one week, and I was meeting with someone else, a woman deeply concerned by the church's silence about evil Trump voters. By not condemning everyone who voted for Trump, we were, she feared, allowing evil to fester unchecked and putting black people at risk.

I responded, "Are you *sure* that *everyone* who voted for Trump is a bodily threat to our black church members?"

She pondered and then nodded. "You don't seem to understand," she said. "*People are dying.* They are dying everywhere at the hands of these Trump supporters. I don't know who will snap next, but I would never let my black friends be alone with a Trump supporter."

I asked, what did she think about my black friends who voted for Donald Trump? And what did she think about black congregants at our church who had forged deep friendships with Trump voters?

She stood firm. These were rare anecdotes. *The Trump voters are out to get them.*

Why Do We Feel So Attacked?

Maybe you're thinking that both sides feel attacked because both sides have become more extreme in their *policy positions*. But is this really true? Are the policy positions of conservatives in 2022 more conservative than they were in 1984? Are the policy positions of liberals in 2022 more liberal than they were in 1984?

Every election year, a survey conducted by the American National Election Studies (ANES) ranks Americans on a policy-extremity index.[1] A score of 1 would mean that the policy positions supported by Democrats and Republicans were extremely far apart. A score of 0 would mean that their policy positions were extremely similar. In 1984, Americans of both parties were as close as they've ever been. We scored a .44 in policy difference. In 2012, Americans were as far apart as they've ever been. We scored a .49.

According to ANES, this is a very small change. Even at our furthest separation, we agree on a lot more than we think.

In other words, if we're polarized, it's *not* because of policy differences. It's *something else*. And whatever is polarizing us, it's bad.

Ongoing research from ANES found that Democrats like Republicans far less today than they did thirty years ago. The same is true for Republicans. Both Democrats and Republicans report that they would be happier with their neighborhood if more people from the opposite political party moved out. Most parents say they would prefer their child marry someone with the same politics more than the same religious beliefs. Employers show noticeable prejudice against job applications from people perceived to be in the other party.[2]

Whatever's polarizing us is causing us to think that our other-partied neighbors are evil, menacing enemies. To understand what's causing the enmity, we need to talk about two groups of fifth graders in the '50s.

How to Flip the Tribal Switch

In the summer of 1954, an academic psychologist named Muzafer Sherif brought two groups of white, middle-class, Protestant boys to Robbers Cave, a camp in southeastern Oklahoma. His goal: observe how the children interact when separated into competitive teams. During the first week, two groups of boys were separated. One group became the Eagles and the other identified themselves as the Rattlers.[3]

During the second week of camp, the Eagles and Rattlers were introduced to each other, and demands for competition quickly began. A day later, they started name-calling. The day after that, they raided each other's camps, threw stones, and accused the other team of cheating. The Eagles stole the Rattlers' flag and burned it. The Rattlers retaliated by stealing the pants of the Eagles' leader, painting them orange and using them as a new flag.

Soon, they were blaming each other for imaginary grievances. The Eagles noticed their watering hole had become cooler overnight and concocted false allegations: the Rattlers had filled it with ice. When the Rattlers found trash on their campsite, they blamed the Eagles. In truth, the Rattlers had simply failed to clean up after *themselves*.

The camp counselors ended the experiment early because they feared the boys would come to blows.

Something happened during the Robbers Cave experiment that's been repeated in labs countless times over the last fifty years: the tribal switch got flipped. Two groups of boys who could have easily become close friends instead became embittered enemies. All it took to flip the tribal switch was a little competition.[4]

But these were fifth-grade boys, right? Surely adults can do better? *We* don't make unnecessary enemies.

A Nation of Eagles and Rattlers

Henri Tajfel, a Polish social psychologist, wanted to build on the Robbers Cave experiment. He posed a question: What was the minimum amount of competition necessary to turn adults against each other?

He began by creating two meaningless groups. Researchers asked participants to estimate the number of dots shown on a screen. After each participant guessed, the researchers *randomly* placed the person into either the "over-estimator group" or the "under-estimator group." None of the participants knew the names or could see the faces of anyone in either group.

The researchers then asked them to choose one of two options:

1. Everyone in both groups could receive the maximum amount of money.

OR

2. The participant's own group could receive less than the maximum amount of money, while the other group could receive even less than them.[5]

The rational choice is the first option. Everyone gets more money, including you and your team. But Tajfel observed that people are not rational by nature. They are tribal. Most participants picked the second option.

Even Tajfel was surprised. He knew group identity mattered but did not expect random, meaningless identities to tribalize people. Ironically, this test was supposed to be the *beginning* of the experiment. He planned to "slowly add conditions until discrimination was achieved."[6] But Tajfel discovered that humans need almost no conditions to discriminate. As soon as people are placed in groups, social identity is formed.

Not only do group members want their team to win—they want to see the other team lose. Lilliana Mason, a political science researcher at Johns Hopkins, put it well: "Even when there is nothing to fight over, group members want to win."[7]

Brain imaging tells the same story. Using functional magnetic resonance imaging (fMRI), neuroscientist David Eagleman discovered that when an adult sees a picture of an in-group member feeling sad, the adult feels sadness with them. But when an adult sees an out-group member feeling sad, the adult experiences *positive* emotions.[8]

Humans are a groupish species. It's our claim to fame (solitary cheetahs can't build cities) and our Achilles' heel (solitary cheetahs also don't build concentration camps). At our best, we focus on what unites us. Jesus gathered wildly diverse people to build his kingdom on earth as in heaven. At our worst, we fixate on what divides us. Nimrod gathered wildly diverse people to build Babel. Our groupishness manufactures incredible good *and* incorrigible grievance.

Conservatives and liberals are not significantly more polarized over policy issues than they were thirty years ago. But we do like each other significantly less. The simple truth is that we pretend to disagree more than we actually do. We've become a nation of Eagles and Rattlers. Our politics now define our social identities. The tribal switch got flipped, and we suddenly find that our limbic-level groupishness is transforming good-willed neighbors into enemies, whose defeat gives us delight.

And all this unnecessary enmity is making your life miserable.

A Beautiful, Strange Friendship

Do you feel happier when loved ones become enemies?

Do you feel joy when you're embattled?

Do communities flourish when neighbors—who share much in common—turn each other into enemies?

In 2019, our church partnered with a progressive documentary film festival to launch a new initiative called the Alethea Project. Together, we planned to bring controversial, progressive films and audiences into evangelical churches like ours in order to create opportunities for conversations between these historically divided groups. We doubted that attendees would change their ethical positions, but we hoped to create mutual understanding, build bridges, and then work collectively toward the common good.

This project grew out of our strange but beautiful friendship with the film festival. More than a decade earlier, our church began supporting a charity fund at the festival. We eventually became one of the festival's largest supporters. And the friendship wasn't just institutional.

People from our church bought passes, attended the festival, and invited friends. People from the festival visited our church. Some of our members joined the festival staff team. Others became super volunteers. Our church's leaders and the festival's leaders were sincere friends.

When people outside of Columbia saw it, they gawked. It was bizarre. The *New York Times* and *Christianity Today* wrote pieces about it. Our unusual friendship tapped into a shared longing to unite across apparently unbridgeable divides.

But let me be clear: we disagreed on a lot.

We built relationships *despite* knowing we disagreed on serious and substantive issues because we took the time to discover that we all shared something greater in common: a desire to see our city flourish. Both parties believed that the growth of arts, culture, and business led to a more vibrant, inclusive, successful city. And we both wanted to support that growth.

> **WE TOOK THE TIME TO DISCOVER THAT WE ALL
> SHARED SOMETHING GREATER IN COMMON:
> A DESIRE TO SEE OUR CITY FLOURISH.**

We never hid our differences. We talked them out. Sometimes it got heated. But we always listened, learned, and sought mutual understanding.

It was beautiful. It was strange. And it was almost over.

How Tribalism Creates Enemies

To launch the Alethea Project, we showed our church a progressive film, *After Tiller*. The film tells the stories of doctors who perform third-term abortions. After the film, we hosted a spirited debate with the filmmakers, the festival, and the church on the topic of abortion. Anyone with an open mind learned something new that night.

While it didn't surprise me that showing the film ruffled the feathers of our church (we are firmly pro-life, after all), I was surprised how much the event angered staff and volunteers at the festival.

I felt confused. What could possibly upset them about showing a pro-abortion film in a church?

After several conversations, I discovered that some of the festival's staff believed that we were *dangerous* to women and society. They felt that the screening and debate loaned credibility to our anti-abortion stance. The festival's leaders were saying, "We may disagree with these people, but they aren't crazy or evil." But the staff disagreed: we were the enemy.

Despite initial tension, the festival and the church moved forward with the project. A year later, we were in New York City, launching the project by screening films at Redeemer Presbyterian Church. The event was a success, and future opportunities looked bright.

At the same time, we were preaching through Genesis at our church. Just two weeks after our NYC screening, we came to the passage in Genesis 1 that says God made humans male and female. This is a controversial passage, but we felt compelled to teach it faithfully. So Keith preached, calling Christians to love our transgender neighbors—some of whom attend our church—while remaining faithful to the Bible's teachings that there are two immutable genders.

We inadvertently stepped on a land mine.

A small group of people—many of whom did not even attend the festival—started a petition demanding that the festival break ties with the church over the sermon. A local art studio we also supported beat them to the punch, releasing a letter condemning the church as transphobic. Sadly, the festival followed suit with a kinder letter that apologized to their staff, volunteers, and community for associating with us and permanently severed the partnership.

I felt terribly for their leadership. Honestly, I don't know if they could have done anything different. Yet it was all so strange because *nothing* had changed about our stance on transgender issues. The festival knew our position years before that sermon. We knew their position. We had candid conversations over our disagreement.

And we agreed that promoting love, kindness, and empathy for all transgender people should be the highest priority. That fundamental agreement allowed us to partner together.

So if no one's outlook changed, what *did* change?

The tribal switch got flipped in our community. People had to pick sides. Differences suddenly mattered more than similarities. Working for shared goals was a damnable compromise. Unity was diabolical. Inner groupishness took over, and long-standing friends needed to be denounced publicly as enemies.

One of the most beautiful, collective relationships in our city came to a close. I'm still grieving it because I don't think our city has felt quite the same since.

Is There Another Way?

After the festival ended our partnership, we knew we had a decision to make. News organizations were calling for our response. Should we fire back? Critique them publicly? Tell our church to boycott the festival? Ask business owners to withdraw their support?

Of course not. Jesus taught us a different way: "You have heard the law that says, 'Love your neighbor' and hate your enemy. But I say, love your enemies! Pray for those who persecute you!"[9]

It wasn't easy, but it *was* simple. Jesus told us what to do: love.

So we took to the internet to thank the festival for our past partnership. I (and others) wrote long social media posts sincerely expressing why we love the festival and encouraging fellow church members to continue attending in the future.

In a private conversation with one of the festival's leaders, he said to me, "It was a master class on grace." I wanted to take credit. But I couldn't. I replied that we're merely students of the master. Jesus founded the one and only tribe whose purpose is to put *other* tribes first. *Especially when it hurts.* Jesus was the first teacher to train his followers to resist their deep-rooted, limbic-level groupishness.

His life is our example. When we were his enemies, he didn't flip the tribal switch. He didn't set out to see us lose—even though we deserved it! By dying for his enemies, Jesus reconciled them to his father.[10] His enemy love created a community out of tribal division.

> ## JESUS FOUNDED THE ONE AND ONLY TRIBE WHOSE PURPOSE IS TO PUT OTHER TRIBES FIRST.

Jesus is calling you into that community. A beautiful, strange community that sets aside its own self-interest. The kind that relinquishes personal advantages. The kind that assumes the best about others and wants the best for them always.

Of course, I fail to live up to this ideal more often than I like to admit. That's because I lack the strength and willpower to love my enemies. It's only when I realize that Jesus has already given me—his onetime enemy—an inexhaustible well of love and that he's promised me ultimate victory over my true enemies—sin, death, and the devil—that I am freed from the desire to exact victories from my perceived enemies in this world, instead offering them a love that is not really my own.

Where is tribalism tempting you to make enemies? How are you tempted to belittle, shame, or scold them? Why do you find loving *that* enemy so difficult? Who is Jesus calling you to love today?

I know it's strange. I know it's hard. But I also know a deeper truth: it's beautiful. And it's beautiful because enemy love is the kind of love that makes Jesus's beauty most visible.

Discussion and Reflection Questions

1. How has tribalism changed the way you see people in the *other* tribe?

2. What makes loving someone in the other tribe difficult for you personally?

3. What about you makes it difficult for someone in the other tribe to love you?

4. Jesus calls you to love your enemies. Who is Jesus calling you to love today?

Chapter 5

TRIBALISM BLINDS YOU

What would make you compromise your most authentic, deeply held values?

After President Clinton lied under oath about having sex with Monica Lewinsky—a tragic, evil abuse of his presidential power—evangelical leaders were quick to condemn him and warn about the social costs of keeping him in office.

Jerry Falwell told *USA Today* that political leaders must "flee from all appearances of evil," especially if they "invoke the name of Christ, as Bill Clinton does."[1] Gary Bauer, former president of the Family Research Council, warned, "These children cannot be set adrift into a culture that tells them that lying is okay, that fidelity is old-fashioned, and that character doesn't count."[2]

Al Mohler, president of the Southern Baptist Convention's flagship seminary, called for Clinton's resignation, writing that "tolerance of serious wrong by leaders sears the conscience of the culture, spawns unrestrained immorality and lawlessness in the society, and surely results in God's judgment." He called "all Americans to embrace and act on the conviction that character does count in public office, and to elect those officials and candidates who, although imperfect, demonstrate consistent honesty, moral purity and the highest character."[3]

No one asked for my opinion, but I honestly think these Christian leaders nailed it. The character of our leaders *does* shape the character of our nation and children. When women are treated as objects, when power is used to manipulate, when future job opportunities are held behind sexual paywalls—the result is a system of sexual oppression and license. Bill Clinton's behavior helped scaffold the abuses uncovered by the #MeToo movement years later.

Character *does* matter.

In the fallout of the Clinton scandal, Focus on the Family founder James Dobson marveled at "the willingness of my fellow citizens to rationalize the President's behavior."[4] Indeed, why are we so willing to turn a blind eye to such grievous acts?

How Tribalism Blinds Us to Truth

Ironically, Dobson found the answer to his own question eighteen years later. In 2016, he endorsed Donald Trump, a thrice-married man who publicly bragged about using his fame to take advantage of women sexually. A man who slept with—and later paid hush money to—a porn star just after his wife gave birth to their son.[5]

How could Dobson rationalize endorsing a man with such a character? He explained that it was because candidate Trump was a "baby Christian" who "speaks in hyperbole."[6] Moreover, Trump supported causes important to Dobson, like putting a pro-life justice on the Supreme Court, and he'd impressed Dobson by granting unprecedented access to Christian leaders, such as televangelist and prosperity gospeler Paula White and Robert Jeffress of Dallas's First Baptist Church.

Indeed, Jeffress—despite writing in 2011 that he rejected the popular idea that "a politician's personal life has no impact on his public service"—said in 2016 that it was incumbent upon Christians to support Trump, whatever his character flaws, because he supported the right causes.[7] In fact, according to Jeffress, candidate Trump's rough and mean demeanor was *exactly* what Christians needed: "I [Jeffress] want the meanest, toughest SOB I can find to protect this nation."[8]

Dobson wasn't the only leader to make an about-face after condemning Clinton. Al Mohler held his ground in 2016, stating publicly that candidate Trump's character made it impossible for Mohler to support him. But in 2020, Mohler changed his tune, arguing that President Trump's sterling record on abortion (among other things) justified voting for him despite his Clinton-like disrespect for and abuse of women.[9]

Let's return to Dobson's 1998 question. Why did Clinton's supporters "rationalize the President's behavior" and argue that he should stay in office? Probably for the same reason President Trump's supporters endorsed him: their behavior was animated by partisan loyalties *more* than their convictions about truth.

But tribalism operates at a deeper level than the rational mind. This means that when tribal allegiances and interests are jeopardized, our reasoning faculties don't resist; they go into hyperdrive—inventing rationalizations for why our tribal desires are the *right desires*.

Tribalism blinds you to the truth. Even truths you once fervently believed. To understand why, I need to share a parable from NYU professor Jonathan Haidt's *The Happiness Hypothesis*.[10]

The Elephant and the Rider

An elephant rider set off to visit his aunt in another town. He mounted the sitting elephant and began shouting and yelling for it to stand. The elephant did not stir. He kicked and punched the elephant. But the elephant stayed put. Finally, he grabbed a stick and hit the elephant. At the exact same moment, the elephant noticed a tree with delicious fruit in the distance, so it stood up and made its way forward toward the fruit.

"Ha!" said the rider to himself. "I knew hitting you would get you going."

Later, they came to a fork in the road. The path on the right led to his aunt's house, and the path on the left led to his mother's house. The rider pointed, tugged, and urged his elephant to go right, but the elephant decided to go left.

When the rider arrived at his mother's house, his mom said, "I thought you were visiting your aunt today, not me." The rider, feeling a bit embarrassed, explained, "That's true. But when I came to the fork in the road, *I decided* I really wanted to see you, and so I came this way."

The Truth about Truth

In the parable, the rider represents your reasoning faculties and the elephant represents your emotional faculties. Ten years ago, I would have told you that I made my decisions rationally and drew my conclusions from evidence and the facts. In other words, for me, *the rider really was in charge of the elephant.*

But my experience as a pastor has wrecked that impression. People follow their hearts, not their heads. The rational mind justifies the heart's desires *after the fact*. Your rider's job is not to *make* decisions but to *explain* decisions. The rider justifies the elephant's choices.

This isn't just a theory. I've seen it happen countless times. Years ago, I knew a guy who strongly affirmed the Bible's sexual ethic: sex brings wholeness and intimacy inside of the context of marriage but causes great harm outside of that context. Then he began dating a girl, and they soon started sleeping together.

A few months later, he admitted that they were having sex but explained that his view on the topic had evolved. There's nothing wrong with premarital sex. He explained that the Bible wasn't very clear on this issue and that, because they were committed to each other exclusively, they were honoring God's design.

Riders don't control elephants. How could they? The rider's job is to rationalize what the elephant wants.

This assessment not only squares with Haidt's research presented in *The Happiness Hypothesis*, but it squares with what the Bible says about our rational minds.

Your reasoning is corrupted and easily justifies corrupt desires.[11] The elephant—your heart—is in charge. You do what you desire most. You become what you love. This means that your most fundamental problem is that your deepest loves are in the wrong order. My friend loved his girlfriend and sexual pleasure *more* than God.

We're all a little like the founder of McDonald's, Ray Kroc, who said, "I believe in God, family, and McDonald's—and in the office *that order is reversed.*"[12] When you love McDonald's more than your family, and your family more than God, something is terribly wrong with your heart.

And your rider will happily rationalize why the disorder is okay.

Jeremiah gave a sober assessment of the human condition: "The heart is deceitful above all things, and desperately sick."[13] It's true. Your elephant is sick, and your rider is deceitful.

But what does all of this have to do with tribalism?

Your elephant loves your tribe. It devours fitting in. It delights in outrage over the other team's problems. Your rider's job is simple. He's not interested in the truth. He's only interested in rationalizing your elephant's tribal hungers.

How Your Rider Works

Have you ever read a blog you disagreed with? According to Adam Grant, Wharton professor of organizational psychology, studies show that it will likely take you longer to read something you disagree with than it takes you to read something you approve of.[14] Why? It's because you're mentally nitpicking details in order to build a counterargument.

In other words, when your elephant disagrees with something, your rider works hard to deconstruct the argument to invalidate it. How? Grant wrote that your inner rider defaults into one of three rationalizing modes when you encounter an argument that challenges your tribe:

> *The Politician:* Your inner politician does not find fault with the argument, but *how* the argument is stated. The politician warns about the *tone* and chastises the argument for unkindness or alienating others. This mode is an expert at tone

policing. "This argument may be right," says the inner politician, "but it's not helping anyone. It's only hurting." Therefore, the argument is invalid.

The Preacher: Your inner preacher is deeply offended by the argument's obvious moral shortcomings. The argument is, in the preacher's view, heretical because it challenges your tribe's orthodoxy—those self-evident truths that cannot be questioned and need not be defended. If the argument itself isn't immoral, the preacher will castigate it for unstated association with other immoral views. Thus, the argument is invalid.

The Prosecutor: Your inner prosecutor builds a case by picking apart every small error in the argument. Rather than consider points with charity, the prosecutor pulls pieces out of their context and reinterprets their meaning with extreme prejudice. The prosecutor finds enough errors (real or imagined) and then declares the argument invalid.[15]

Which mode does your rider most prefer? Personally, my rider is a big-time prosecutor who does a little preaching on the side.

Unfortunately, your inner politician, preacher, and prosecutor make your life miserable. They prevent you from learning and listening with charity and agitate you into anxious, outraged case building. Rather than seeing people (and their perspectives) as complex mixtures of right and wrong, truth and falsehood, your rider treats them as threats to be shamed and eliminated. Your rider's job is to blind you to the truth on the other side, so long as that feeds your elephant's desires.

And your sin-sick elephant loves its tribe more than truth.

Is there any hope? If the rider can't control the elephant, and the elephant loves tribe over truth, are we doomed to unending tribalism?

How to Become a Truth Lover

Before a single primary ballot was cast, almost no one predicted that Donald Trump would win the Republican presidential nomination. Almost no one except Jean-Pierre Beugoms, who shocked his fellow analysts by giving Trump a whopping 68 percent chance of winning the primary.[16]

Jean-Pierre is what's called a "superforecaster," an elite analyst who repeatedly predicts the future accurately. So what's his secret?

To show you, I need to explain why—after nailing the Republican primary—Jean-Pierre *botched* the 2016 election. Like most analysts, he predicted that Hillary Clinton would win. After the election, he revisited his process to determine why he had failed, and he came up with a startlingly simple answer:

He didn't want Donald Trump to win the presidency.[17]

As a result, Jean-Pierre subconsciously prioritized data and statistical models that favored Clinton. He vowed to never make the same mistake again. How?

Jean-Pierre began to build his sense of personal worth on *seeking truth*, not loyalty to the left. He realized that the more he identified with Democrats, the more unreliable his results would become. Conversely, the more he loved accuracy, the more accurate his predictions would become.

Jean-Pierre reordered his loves. He trained his elephant to love truth more than tribe. In fact, he began to identify with a *new* tribe: the superforecasters. Membership in that tribe—which required accuracy—mattered more to him than membership in the Democratic tribe.

In other words, Jean-Pierre retrained his elephant to love truth. He redirected his elephant's tribal longings toward a tribe that loved truth. This set his rider free *to speak truth and know truth.*

What Are Your Deepest Loves?

In our podcast interview, Justin Giboney, Christian author, political strategist, and cofounder of the And Campaign, told us he attended the 2012 Democratic National Convention as a voting delegate.[18] At that convention, there was a motion to take "God" out of the Democratic platform, but Justin knew he could not support this. So he spoke truth to power. And he hasn't stopped. While Justin identifies as a Democrat, he is quite willing to challenge Democrats on issues like abortion. Why? Justin's loves are in the right order. His loyalty to the lamb supersedes his loyalty to the donkey. And because his elephant wanted the right thing, his rider gave him the power to speak truth.

Are your loves in the right order? Does your love for the lamb transcend your love for the donkey or the elephant?

The apostle Paul wrote that every human heart is disordered: "[Humans] exchanged the glory of the immortal God for images made to look like a mortal human being and birds and animals and reptiles."[19]

Humans love created things more than God. And of course, most Christians know that we can be tempted to love money, possessions, comfort, pleasure, prestige, approval, control, and romance more than Jesus. But many forget that we can just as easily love our *tribe* more than Jesus.

> ## ARE YOUR LOVES IN THE RIGHT ORDER? DOES YOUR LOVE FOR THE LAMB TRANSCEND YOUR LOVE FOR THE DONKEY OR THE ELEPHANT?

Paul said that the consequence of disordered love is a disordered life: "God gave them over to a depraved mind, so that they do what ought not to be done. They have become filled with every kind of wickedness, evil, greed and depravity. They are full of envy, murder, strife, deceit and malice. They are gossips, slanderers, God-haters, insolent, arrogant and boastful; they invent ways of doing evil; they disobey their parents."[20]

This means that one of the easiest ways to determine if our love is disordered is to look at our actions. So do a self-assessment. When someone from a different tribe shares their perspective, do you:

- Feel a sense of anger, or even malice, toward them?
- Feel a sense of confident, arrogant superiority over them during or after the fact?
- State "facts" that you are not sure are true in order to deceitfully win the argument?

- Gossip about that person after the debate ends?
- Slander that person's faith or character after the debate ends?

According to Paul, these are signs of disordered love. But there is hope.

Paul also said that those who turn away from the idols they love more than God will not only be forgiven, they'll be transformed.[21]

You cannot force your elephant to love Jesus most, but Jesus can.[22] His Spirit can supernaturally transform your desires so that Jesus comes first. He can give you membership in Jesus's tribe so that your desires for belonging drive you toward truth and obedience, not partisan tribalism.

Living this out is a *process* of ongoing self-assessment and continual turning back to Jesus. In other words, there is a partnership between you and Jesus. He supplies you the strength and the grace, but you also must walk in that grace.

The more you resist allegiance to a political tribe, the more you'll embrace Jesus's kingdom. The more you listen *charitably* to an opposing view, the more you'll heed Jesus's voice. The more you assume the best about others, the more you can assume you're walking in God's grace.

THE MORE YOU ASSUME THE BEST ABOUT OTHERS, THE MORE YOU CAN ASSUME YOU'RE WALKING IN GOD'S GRACE.

When your elephant—your heart—loves Jesus above all else, your rider—your rational mind—will be set free to use your rational powers for good. Instead of rationalizing wrongheaded ideas, your rider will resist lies and speak words of truth, justice, nobility, mercy, and goodness, all to the glory of God.

Discussion and Reflection Questions

1. When your rider (your rational mind) is defending the choices of your elephant (your heart), does your rider go into politician mode, preacher mode, or prosecutor mode?

2. What are signs that you've entered into politician, preacher, or prosecutor mode? Practically, what steps can you take to resist?

3. What are the tribal idols your elephant is tempted to love more than God? How is God calling you to reorder your loves and put him first?

Part Two

Why We're Tribal

Does it feel like tribalism is *everywhere?*

In part 1, you saw how tribalism is hurting you. Now you'll pull back the camera to look at how your cultural moment is fomenting tribalism nationwide. No one is an island, after all. You are part of a cultural continent, and its topography shapes your experience.

In part 2, you'll analyze your culture by exploring how human sin corrupts human minds and drives people toward tribalism (chapter 6). After that, you'll discover how social media encourages tribalism (chapter 7), how the loss of truth entrenches tribalism (chapter 8), and how social erosion catalyzes tribalism (chapter 9).

As you read these chapters, our prayer is that Jesus will give you eyes to see your cultural landscape and the power to resist its tribalizing influence.

In part 2, we refer to conversations with John Mark Comer and Mark Sayers. If you want access to those interviews in full (and you should, because they're both brilliant), scan the QR code below.

Chapter 6

Why Your Brain Is Tribal

Astronaut Jeff Ashby will never forget the first time he looked at Earth from his seat on the space shuttle *Columbia*:

> My first glimpse of the Earth from space was about fifteen minutes into my first flight, when I looked up from my checklist and suddenly we were over the lit part of the Earth with our windows facing down. Below me was the continent of Africa, and it was moving by much as a city would move by from an airline seat. Circling the entire planet in ninety minutes … you can easily from space see the connection between someone on one side of the planet to someone on the other—and there are no borders evident. So it appears as just this one common layer that we all exist in.[1]

Ashby said that his perspective on the world was forever altered. All the boundaries we think divide us—national, civic, political, racial—are imaginary. What we share in common is far greater. You live on the same planet as 7 billion other humans. You breathe the same air. Drink the same water.

Yet this is a reality we rarely consider. Even the most trivial things divide us. In 2019, a Twitter user created a map using geo-tagged data to show the most hated NFL teams in every state.[2]

The map shows that fans are surprisingly homogenous in their NFL hatred. I live in a region of five states that all hate the Patriots. Maybe you live in an area that hates the Cowboys, or the Seahawks, or the 49ers. Wherever you live, the people around you likely agree on what team to root against as much as what team to root for.

Wharton professor Adam Grant and doctoral student Tim Kundro ran a test that showed sports fans assumed negative stereo-types about fans of rival teams. When asked why they disliked fans of their rivals, they gave alarmingly rational reasons: fans of the rival team were obnoxious, loud, annoying, cocky, dumb, rude, arrogant, entitled, vulgar, disrespectful, cheaters, braggers, losers, and worse.[3]

It's not just sports. Another study asked people whether a hot dog is a sandwich.[4] After participants answered, they were given two choices:

1. Give $3 to everyone who agrees with me and $4 to everyone who disagrees.
2. Give $2 to everyone agrees with me and $1 to everyone who disagrees.

More than 71 percent of participants picked option number 2. We would rather lose money than give people who think a hot dog is a sandwich more money. Just for the record, a hot dog is *not* a sandwich.

This problem escalates the more deeply we identify with a tribal group, be it regional, socioeconomic, vocational, racial, or political.

The 7 billion people on planet Earth don't just share the same air; we share a similar way of thinking. Like it or not, the human brain has not changed tremendously in the last 35,000 years. We navigate our world with the same set of mental faculties as ancient hunter-gatherers, banded together in small tribes.

Where You Got Your Tribal Mind

Imagine that you're living in the Stone Age, before writing and agriculture. You have simple tools and weapons made of wood and stone. You spend your days foraging berries and hunting food for you and your small band to eat. Your tribe is nomadic, setting up and tearing down small camps in search of calories.

The threats to your collective life are tremendous: predators, weather, and food shortages. But there are also human threats.

Some are internal: the freeloaders who eat your food but provide no utility. An extra, unproductive mouth to feed puts everyone at risk of hunger and even starvation. Conversely, if you become a freeloader, your tribe might very well leave you behind.

Some are external: the *other* tribe camping nearby. Will they lay claim to the food your tribe so desperately needs? If they go hungry, will they raid your camp for supplies and murder your family? If you build an alliance with a member of a different tribe, will your own tribe become suspicious of you?

Thus, your survival depends largely on three social things:

1. Tightly bonding with your own tribe
2. Showing healthy suspicion toward outsiders
3. Not freeloading

The most successful tribes were those in which everyone worked collectively for the common good and showed empathy to insiders. These tribes demonstrated solidarity by participating in the same rituals, sharing the same beliefs, practicing loyalty to group members, avoiding the same taboos, and dressing and speaking in the same ways.

A sense of belonging wasn't just good for the heart; it was good for the stomach.

The most successful tribes were also wary of outsiders. When another tribe got too close, they set up sentinels to keep watch against raids. Occasionally, they bartered for goods and, on rare occasions, merged to face a bigger threat (perhaps a bigger tribe). But more often than not, combat was more beneficial than cooperation. Destroying another tribe might open new opportunities for hunting and foraging. Pillaging their goods might earn you enough food to live another day.

Now multiply this by hundreds of generations. Tribes without suspicion and solidarity weaken and die off. The most united and suspicious tribes survive and thrive. They pass on their minds and cultures to the next generation.

Of course, that was *then*, and this is *now*. Surely modern people can give up our groupishness and become citizens of the world, just as Jeff Ashby—the astronaut we quoted at the beginning of this chapter—imagined? Unfortunately, it's not that easy. We're not the descendants of astronauts; we're the descendants of Stone Age survivors. And modern science proves the point.

The Love Drug and Mirror Neurons

A few years back, news stories started popping up about a chemical produced in the human brain that elevated empathy, connection, and love: oxytocin. This is the chemical released when a mother and child see each other for the first time. It's what a man and woman secrete when they're madly in love. It's what you're missing when the relationship feels dry.

But oxytocin doesn't just function on an individual level. It also works on a group level. Our brains release oxytocin during intense group experiences: whether it's teenagers at a rave, an aboriginal tribe dancing in unison, a military squad marching in synchronicity, or a congregation worshipping collectively.

So could we fix the world if we added a little oxytocin into the water? No, because oxytocin isn't just the love drug; it's also the tribal drug.

Carsten De Dreu, a professor of social and organizational psychology at Leiden University, divided men into two groups.[5] He and his colleagues sprayed oxytocin into one group's nostrils but not the other. The men in the oxytocin group made less selfish decisions if it helped out their own group. But did it lead them to be more selfless toward people in the other group? No. As it turns out, the men with oxytocin were more likely to harm outsiders. Oxytocin increases group cohesion *and* suspicion of outsiders.

So is there a way to increase empathy toward outsiders? This leads us to mirror neurons.

Mirror neurons reflect the emotions of other people inside your brain. When you see someone smile, your mirror neurons make you feel like you're smiling. If you see someone in pain, your mirror neurons help you to share it.

But there's a catch.

Psychologist and neuroscientist Tania Singer discovered that mirror neurons fire only when we see people we like: people who look like us, dress like us, think like us, or share some other identity with us.[6] When we see someone from an out-group, they stop working. In fact, Singer's study suggests that we experience the inverse feelings of outsiders, especially if they are doing something we disapprove of. If they feel happy, we feel agitation. If they feel pain, we feel relief.

When we put it all together, a clear picture emerges: you have an incredible, innate capacity to love your in-group neighbor, but an equally innate capacity to disdain your out-group enemy.

WE'RE NOT THE DESCENDANTS OF ASTRONAUTS; WE'RE THE DESCENDANTS OF STONE AGE SURVIVORS.

All of this explains why it's so easy to trust someone in your tribe and doubt someone outside of it. You have a biological predisposition. It also explains why breaking with your tribe's perspective can be incredibly painful. It sets off your internal, tribal alert system: *If I do this, I risk exclusion from my group. If I do this, I risk their disdain. If I do this, I might go hungry and die alone.*

Choosing truth over tribe costs a lot more than admitting "I was wrong." It may cost you friendships, family, credibility, or social capital. People who once mirrored your emotional state may suddenly become suspicious of it. Those with whom you once felt a deep bond suddenly seem separated by a chasm.

Our primal, limbic selves want to resist at all costs. Your inner elephant is freaking out. It knows that going solo only works in John Wayne movies, not in real life.

Why Picking the Right Tribe Matters

We've been critical of tribalism throughout this book, but this chapter begs a deeper question: Can we really escape tribalism at all? Is it *too* hardwired into our biology?

I will leave it to theologians, biologists, and ethicists to parse out the details, but given the evidence, here's my unacademic conclusion:

> God designed us to be empathetic creatures who have an amazing, innate, social capacity to cohere into groups who collectively pursue the common good. But humanity redefined good and evil in the Garden of Eden. This included rejecting God's vision of a worldwide human tribe where all people are understood as his image bearers and imbued with inestimable worth and value. Instead, we drew tribal lines. Ethnic lines. Socioeconomic lines. Cultural lines. Political lines. National lines.

By choosing division over unity, we unleashed a
dark inversion of our innate empathic capacities:
suspicion, disdain, and violence. As a result, every
living human is both a glory and a ruin. We can
experience both the heights of selflessness and the
depths of prejudice.

Tribalism in a world unmarred by sin could be a beautiful
thing. But you do not live in that world. In our world, tribalism is
a powerful tool for creating coalitions that fuel disdain. This is why
partisans, demagogues, and supporters of "-isms" all speak the language of twisted tribalism. They talk about "us" and "them." They
choose outrage over charity. They cheer when an opponent falls and
cry foul when one of their own takes a tumble.

EVERY LIVING HUMAN IS BOTH A GLORY AND A RUIN.

Again, on one level there is no way to escape tribalism. It's
hardwired into your biology for a good purpose! But that doesn't
mean you can't resist the dark side of tribalism. How? By consciously
choosing to embrace the *right* tribe. If you choose the wrong group,
your tribal instincts will be bent toward harm, but if you choose the
right group, your instincts might bend toward what is true, good,
and beautiful. Let me explain.

The Hope of the World

In our podcast interview with Christian thinker and author John
Mark Comer, he told me, "The great hope of the church right now

is young people of color all over the world."[7] Statistically, he's right. Christianity is growing rapidly in countries like Malaysia, China, Brazil, Kenya, and Nigeria—even as it shrinks in the West.

But that comment also served as a reminder to me of why Jesus's tribe is the only tribe that produces empathy, love, and charity for all people. It's because it's the only tribe *for* all people. It does not matter whether you're a man or woman or trans or gender queer. It does not matter if you're straight or gay. It does not matter if you're Australian, Taiwanese, Ugandan, or Colombian. It does not matter whether you're a libertarian, communist, or nationalist.

Jesus's tribe is the *only* tribe that is literally open to everyone. Of course, our allegiance to Jesus will relativize our allegiance to all the other tribes in the world. Of course, it will change us. But this is the only club that has *no* prerequisites or prequalifications. King Jesus simply calls you to turn from your old allegiances and give your ultimate allegiance to him.

This deeply offended the tribal coalitions of Jesus's day. They wanted him to pick a side. *Jesus, are you a Pharisee, a Sadducee, a Roman sympathizer, a Zealot, or an Essene?* But he refused to join their tribes. He infuriated them by calling people from every group to follow him. He called Matthew, the Roman sympathizer and tax collector. He called Simon, the Zealot committed to guerrilla warfare against Rome. He called prostitutes to be his disciples, Pharisees like Nicodemus, wealthy women like Joanna, and social bottom dwellers like Bartimaeus.

This is the beauty of Jesus's tribe. It's for *everyone*. And it's *for* everyone.

If you follow Jesus faithfully, you will be slowly set free from the suspicion, disdain, and hatred that characterize every other tribe, without losing the cohesion, empathy, and solidarity that we all long to experience. In fact, I hesitate to call Jesus followers a tribe, because this group is so different from all the other cultural coalitions that go by the same name. And yet, I know it is a tribe, and I'm grateful that he welcomed me into it.

You don't get to choose whether you're tribal, so choose your tribe carefully.

Discussion and Reflection Questions

1. How can you tell the difference between healthy and unhealthy tribalism?

2. How does sin corrupt the good aspects of tribalism (belonging, shared purpose, shared identity)?

3. How is Jesus's tribe—the church—different from other tribes? Do you see those differences reflected in your life?

Chapter 7

Why Your Facebook Feed Is Tribal

Mary Ann Luna met one of her closest friends at work thirty years ago. For fifteen years, they ate lunch together almost every day. They vacationed together. They celebrated together. Their friendship gave them both a deep sense of security and belonging.[1]

But all of that was about to change.

For thirty years, they talked work and family and life — never politics. For example, despite living in a border state, they never talked about immigration. Both knew and worked alongside immigrants without giving it much thought. But now her friend was sending links to story after story detailing violence committed by immigrants. Mary Ann slowly got the sense that something was pulling them apart.

She was right. A man had come between them.

Donald J. Trump.

Mary Ann's friend had fallen in (political) love with Donald Trump when he won the Republican nomination and faced Hillary Clinton in the 2016 presidential election. Seemingly out of nowhere, her longtime friend began to spend hours every day reading articles attacking Clinton and praising Trump on social media. She forwarded her favorites to Mary Ann.

Eventually, Mary Ann asked her friend to stop talking about the election—she wasn't that interested in politics anyway—but her friend seemed unable to resist. She continued to send Facebook posts and articles from sources that Mary Ann found questionable. If Mary Ann ever questioned Trump, her friend would become defensive, demanding sources, and scolding her for listening to elite, dishonest news sources.

After the 2016 election, things never quite felt the same. But they resumed their lunches and tried to repair their friendship.

When the cycle began to repeat itself in 2020, a more permanent distance grew between them. Mary Ann stopped opening her friend's emails and texts. She was exhausted by the constant stream of negativity. After a month of mutual silence, in late November of 2020, Mary Ann sent her a text: "I am sorry that your guy lost, but let's leave politics out and just be friends."[2]

Mary Ann never heard back. Had she been dumped for Trump? Ghosted for ghosting on politics?

Maybe the answer to all three questions is yes. But that's only half of the story. The other half took place hundreds of miles away from their daily lunches, in Palo Alto, California.

From Social Media to Social Breakdown

Think of the most politically extreme person you know. Have they always been that way, or have you noticed a change in the last five years? Do they send you articles that make you scratch your head and wonder, *Where do they find this stuff?* Do they say things about the other side that make you think, *That seems a little extreme*?

Do you discover that they seem alarmingly unaware of alternative perspectives or of events that contradict their political narratives?

If so, chances are it started on social media. And this isn't by accident; it's by design.

In a 2018 presentation by Facebook, one slide read, "Our algorithms exploit the human brain's attraction to divisiveness … in an effort to gain user attention and increase time on the platform."[3] It sounds like a harebrained plot from a Scooby-Doo villain aiming to destroy the world.

But this isn't a cartoon. It's reality. And the plot is *working*.

In the beginning, neither Google nor Facebook sought to destroy society. But they both shared a problem: how to monetize their service without charging users. Just ask yourself, how much did you pay Google to allow you to use its engine? Nothing. Doesn't that seem odd? Google owns the keys to the greatest information and knowledge dispensary in human history, but it charges less than a subscription to the *New York Times*. How?

What about Meta and its subsidiaries, Facebook, WhatsApp, and Instagram? How much do you pay to stay connected to millions of people and the content they create and share? *Nothing.* Meta owns the most powerful and pervasive social connection tools ever invented, but it charges less than your cell phone carrier does.

This should raise a question too few people ask: How did corporations, offering extraordinary services to their customers for *free*, become some of the wealthiest corporations in the world?

The answer is simple: You *aren't* the customer. *You're the product.*

How Big Tech Got Big: The Google Story

In *The Age of Surveillance Capitalism*, Shoshana Zuboff explains how Google and Meta grew from unprofitable start-ups into two of the biggest tech companies in the world.[4]

For many people, Google is synonymous with the internet, but the search company arrived on the scene nearly a decade after the internet became widely available. When they launched, a vast supply of information existed online, but there was no quality way to search it. To solve that problem, Google sent web crawlers across the entirety of the internet. Like tiny little spiders, the web crawlers scoured pages to create and organize a comprehensive model of the internet. Thus, when you asked Google a question, Google knew *exactly* where to find the answer.[5]

But Google had a problem: they generated virtually no profits.

The solution to their profit problem changed the landscape of the internet far more than their search engine ever did. In the same way they created a model of the internet, Google set out to create a digital model of *you*. They realized that if they tracked your searches, the websites you visit, where you linger, what you buy, where you live, and how long it takes you to make a purchase, they would know the perfect way to sell you something. What sells *you* on a product? A video? A graphic? A text box? Do you respond to masculine ads? To a company that supports your cause? Do you impulse buy after emotive ads? Do you need a long blog to give you a sense that you've researched your product? Do you need customer reviews?

Even if you don't know the answers to these questions, I assure you, Google knows.

By building a model of your online purchase habits, Google realized they could give an advertiser's sales team something better than a warm lead. Google could give them a curated road map straight into your wallet. Using Google's advertising platform, advertisers are able to tailor their approach to each individual customer. Google makes sure the right ad hits the right customer at the right moment, landing the advertiser a sale.

But building a model of *you* isn't easy. It requires a level of surveillance that would make the Chinese Communist Party blush. Google, however, was unphased. How do they build a model of you?

They surveil, record, and compile *everything* you do on the internet.

They used cars with cameras attached to them to map neighborhoods and identify every router name and internet access point in almost every American neighborhood.

They launched an email platform where they could legally read, record, and store all your emails.

They developed a GPS app that knows where you live, where you shop, where you get gas, where you hang out, who you hang out with, and where you work.

They developed a smartphone operating system that tracks everything you do across every single app.

I know people who think their phone is spying on them, because when they talk about something they never previously searched online, they suddenly start seeing ads for it. Your phone is *not* spying on you (yet). Something far more remarkable is happening: Google is using machine learning and their ever-developing model of you to *predict* what you want before you even know you want it. Your phone isn't spying on you. It's guessing, and it knows so much about you, most of its guesses are correct.

> *Your phone isn't spying on you. It's guessing, and it knows so much about you, most of its guesses are correct.*

More darkly, Google and Facebook can use ads and articles to *change* what you want and shape what you think. Big Brother, it turns out, isn't a violent totalitarian. He surveils you covertly, sells you sweetly, and manipulates you gently. So gently that you don't even notice.

How Big Tech Got Big: The Meta Story

Meta—which owns Facebook, Instagram, and WhatsApp—was the next Big Tech company to begin surveillance operations on the public. It tapped into a treasure trove of data that Google could only dream about.[6]

Meta knows your spouse, children, friends, and family.

Meta knows where you vacation, what you like to drink and eat, and what you wear.

Meta knows when you wake up and go to sleep.

Meta knows what makes you angry, happy, and sad.

Meta knows what kind of ads grab your attention. Video, text, graphics, bikinis, models, cars, flowers, food, whatever.

But maybe you don't have Facebook or Instagram or WhatsApp. Or maybe you don't spend much time on them, at least. Surely, *you're* okay. Nope. Meta still surveils you. Meta is quietly integrated into most other websites, allowing it to track your activity in countless other places.

In other words, Meta, just like Google, is making a comprehensive model of *you*. This means they can promise advertisers the eyes of people already interested and predisposed to consume their content and purchase their product.

As with Google, you aren't Meta's customer. You're their product. And there's a good chance both corporations know you better than you do.

The key, for Meta, is keeping you on their platforms for two reasons. First, the more time you spend on Facebook or Instagram, the better their model of you gets. The better their model gets, the better they can sell your attention to advertisers.

Second, when you leave Facebook or Instagram, they can no longer sell your attention. Thankfully, keeping you on the platform is relatively simple. Using lessons learned from casinos, they offer variable rewards (likes, comments), a glittering array of changing images, and of course, the most important ingredient: *emotion*.

Which takes us back to their shockingly honest slide: "Our algorithms exploit the human brain's attraction to divisiveness ... in an effort to gain user attention and increase time on the platform."

In other words, Meta is hacking the worst parts of our innate tribalism to the tune of billions of dollars in profit.

Outrage for Profit

Which headline would you most likely click?

> *1. Joe Biden steals trillions of taxpayer dollars to indoctrinate YOUR children.*
>
> *2. Five reasons conservatives are stonewalling Biden's plan to rescue children out of poverty and the implicit racism driving their efforts.*
>
> *3. An overview of pros and cons to Joe Biden's new plan to help families.*

If you're exhausted by all the online politics, you might pick option 3. But Meta and Google know that anger keeps you on their platforms, so they're both much more likely to offer you option 1 or 2.[7]

Anger is a heady experience, after all. We love the rush of self-righteous indignation. It was the default emotion of Jesus's most frustrated opponents. Meta desperately wants to befriend your inner Pharisee because tribalism isn't a bug in its business strategy—it is the business strategy.

Unfortunately, the longer people spend on these platforms, the more extreme they get. It's a vicious loop. They're serviced outrageous headlines. At first, they scoff. Then they believe. Which makes even more outrageous posts seem more credible. Which of course makes the next one more believable. And on it goes.

Keeping people angry simply requires an ever-increasing level of shrill, partisan hot takes—both from media and from the people you follow. Over time, innumerable rabbit holes open up and descend into an ever-darkening well of conspiracies, outlandish academic theories, and alternative facts that collectively begin to construct a new mental reality.

This explains why your friends and family are becoming more radicalized on the internet. *Big Tech is serving them more and more radical content in a bid for their attention.* Your friends are the product Meta sells to their advertisers. Your friends' outrage is the addictive nicotine hit that keeps them coming back. The personal and social consequences don't matter, as long as it's profitable.

You Are the Product

It's incredibly unnerving to realize that your personal information is auctioned off to advertisers. It's more unnerving to understand that this incentivizes Big Tech to tear down social trust and fuel outrage. I doubt this is their conscious intention. They just want money. And the rest of us—who have little to gain from the culture wars—suffer social dissolution.

The next time an ad, video, article, or blog post invites you to assume the worst about the other tribe, just ask yourself: "Is this real, or am I just a product for sale to the highest bidder? Is the other tribe evil, or is an algorithm manipulating my basest emotions?"

Unfortunately, this kind of thinking is not our default. The deck is stacked against us. Your mind is hardwired for tribalism. Artificial intelligence is hardwired for profits. Is it any surprise that Space Age technology is capitalizing on our Stone Age minds?

The Powers, the World, and You

No one likes to admit that they're being manipulated. It makes you feel childish. But in this case, the problem is not childishness. The problem is that there are forms of manipulation that are so incredibly subtle, complex, and alluring that no one—not even the adults in the room—is unaffected.

Jesus understood this. While he lacked the technical language to describe systems whose structures manipulate, divide, and spread evil, he did use one term that summed up this entire idea: "the world."

For Jesus, "the world" was a phrase that summarized the complex way human sin and idolatry folds itself into cultures, institutions, and political organizations. These interlocking forces create an overwhelming system that structurally tempts people away from God, disincentivizes righteousness, promotes lies, and justifies evil.[8]

Jesus said he is not "of this world," meaning that the kingdom he brings to earth is not polluted by evil, injustice, or idolatry.[9] The kingdom of God is the system and structure that develop when human and divine goodness, faith, and worship fold themselves into human cultures and institutions.

You do not live fully in the kingdom yet. You have one foot firmly in "the world." Which means that you need to make a sober self-assessment. *You can be manipulated.* In fact, if Jesus is right about the world, it's more accurate to say that *you are being manipulated.* And you are unwittingly participating in the manipulation of others.

In the twenty-first century, it's hard to imagine a more monstrous articulation of "the world" than what Big Tech is doing to families and communities. This does not mean that it cannot be stopped or changed. That's my prayer, though I won't pretend to know how it will happen. Pandora's box is open; there's no going back.

But my personal responsibility is not to solve that problem. It is to be sober minded on the internet and know that Jesus commanded me not to be controlled by the world. That tribal headline is not in charge of my mind. That advertisement is not in charge of my pocketbook. That outrageous post is not in charge of my emotions. *Jesus is.*

> **MY PERSONAL RESPONSIBILITY IS TO BE SOBER MINDED ON THE INTERNET AND KNOW THAT JESUS COMMANDED ME NOT TO BE CONTROLLED BY THE WORLD.**

You will never plumb the depths of how the world is manipulating you—and how Big Tech is doing it specifically. Nonetheless, you will never experience an inch of freedom from that manipulative power if you continue to live by the lie that it's *not* having an impact on your life. It is.

Be not of this world. Instead, seek in your own way to build an outpost of the kingdom on earth as in heaven.

Discussion and Reflection Questions

1. How has social media impacted your relationships negatively? Has it caused conflict in your family or at your workplace?

2. How has social media fed tribalism in your life? Has social media made you more or less Christlike?

3. How does understanding Facebook and Google's business model—selling *you* as a product to advertisers—change how you want to interact with their platforms?

4. Social media is not designed to surface truth and sink falsehood, but instead to surface the sensational and sink nuance. How does knowing this change how you read things on social media? How would Jesus discern truth and falsehood online if he were you?

Chapter 8

WHY YOUR PERSONAL TRUTH IS TRIBAL

The second presidential election between John Adams and Thomas Jefferson was toxically polarized. Jefferson's proxies accused Adams of being a "bald, blind, crippled, toothless" man who wanted to start a war with France.[1] Adams's party fired back. They claimed that if Thomas Jefferson won, "murder, robbery, rape, adultery, and incest will be openly taught and practiced, the air will be rent with the cries of the distressed, the soil will be soaked with blood, and the nation black with crimes."[2]

Looking at political ads today, I know that Mark Twain got it right: "History doesn't repeat itself; it rhymes."

But if the polarization of our era is a rhyme, it's a slant rhyme. It's similar, and yet entirely different.

Enlightenment optimism shaped the Jeffersonian era. It was a time when the brightest thinkers were optimistic about human reason's capacity to discover the Truth about reality. This was "capital T" truth. Universal Truth that was true for all people in all times and all places. This kind of truth impinged on everyone—no matter their race, gender, or creed.

But the Enlightenment failed. And we're still living in its ruins.

Today, you're less likely to hear people talk about "the truth" than "my truth." During my time working in college ministry, I watched more and more students deny the reality of Universal Truth. This is called relativism. It's the idea that where you stand depends on where you sit. Your understanding of truth is subjective and rooted *wholly* in your perspective. "I have *my* truth. You have *your* truth. And one is not better (or truer) than the other."

In Jefferson's era, politicians bandied over *the* truth. Today, there is a competitive market of alternative truths. The battle is not to define truth but to have the power to actualize *your tribe's* truth.

These alternative truths come in many forms, but the most popular variety are abstract, unprovable theories, such as critical theory and conspiracy theories. One comes from the ivory tower of academia, and the other from the internet underbelly of 4chan. (Please don't Google search 4chan or visit its site. Because when I say it's the underbelly of the internet, I mean it's the pornographic proprietor of disturbing images, disgusting ideas, and damnable conspiracy theories.) Both critical theory and conspiracy theories want their truth to rule the world. Both theories deny objective reality. Both theories invite you into a Ferris wheel of circular logic that, once entered, is difficult to exit.

And both theories offer profoundly tribal visions of truth.

Critical Theory
Why 2 + 2 = 5

"Actually, two plus two *can* equal five." Lily spoke with such earnestness that I almost believed her. We were discussing whether "capital T" truth existed. I suggested that "two plus two equals four" might be such a truth. She disagreed.

"Imagine there are four factories." Lily began drawing on a napkin. "Two are owned by Company A, and two are owned by Company B. Company A has one machine in one of its factories and one and a half machines in the other. Company B also has one machine in one of its factories and one and a half machines in the other."

She looked up at me triumphantly, as though I would understand her point. I did not. So she continued, "If the two companies merged their two factories, you would call that two plus two, right?"

I nodded. Then Lily explained her point: "But if the two companies merged, they would own five machines total, not four. See! Two plus two equals five."

"That's not right," I responded. "You just added up machines, not factories. Two and a half machines plus two and a half machines equals five machines. Two factories plus two factories still only equals four factories."

I have to admit that my tone wasn't very gracious. I felt exasperated. Were we really arguing over simple math?

Lily did not believe me. She assured me that what I had said was *my* truth. She, for her part, would hold to *her* truth. For her, there is no qualitative difference between these statements: "two plus two equals four" and "ramen is the best kind of noodle." *Both* are matters of personal taste.

After our conversation, Lily sent me the work of Illinois mathematics professor Dr. Rochelle Gutiérrez to prove her point.[3] Dr. Gutiérrez argued in a plenary paper that traditional mathematics (what you learned in school) comes out of "Whitestream" culture and is an expression of "global White supremacy." Rather than privileging "Whitestream" math, Dr. Gutiérrez recommended that educators should train students in traditional forms of math found in indigenous populations. Of course, these forms do not allow for the complex computation required to build bridges and buildings or to code software, but that's a small price to pay.

But what's most important to Dr. Gutiérrez is that no form of math be elevated as superior to a different form. She worried that training children in "Whitestream" math engrains white ways of thinking, which are toxic for children.

Unfortunately, her work glossed over the historical fact that modern math is *not* the proprietary invention of white Europeans. "Whitestream" mathematics first developed in Neo-Babylonian, Chinese, and Arabic cultures.

WHEN _EVERYTHING_ BOILS DOWN TO PERSONAL TASTE, TRUTH LOSES ITS FLAVOR.

Eventually, I asked to meet with Lily again, but the conversation wasn't very fruitful. When you can't agree that two plus two equals four is objectively true, it's difficult to agree on anything. When *everything* boils down to personal taste, truth loses its flavor.

Fat Studies

A doctor is seeing a patient who is dangerously overweight. She tells him, "If you don't lose some weight, you're risking heart disease, kidney failure, and liver problems."

Do you think this doctor is oppressing her patient? Shaming him? Stealing his power to define health for himself?

According to a new branch of critical theory called "fat studies," the answer is yes. Fat studies is not, as you might expect, the scientific study of obesity. It is the study of how society—including doctors—uses language to oppress and marginalize obese people.

According to experts in fat studies, medical knowledge is *not* rooted in biological truth. Instead, medicine is a social construct. Doctors define "healthy" in ways that oppress and demean those who fall outside the definition. As a result, medical professionals gain power, prestige, and wealth, sweeping patients they deem unhealthy to the margins of society.[4]

It hasn't taken long for this trend to catch on culturally. *Cosmopolitan* put photos of obese models on its cover with the caption "This is healthy." But is it really healthy? There are piles of objective studies showing that obesity causes many serious, life ending diseases. Unfortunately, experts in fat studies call this objective research "fat shaming."

There's no doubt in my mind that Americans show unkindness toward women who do not fit the (equally unhealthy!) stereotype of rail-thin models who normally populate *Cosmo*'s covers. That prejudice is real and it's worth critiquing! But dubbing medical advice as "fat shaming" is tantamount to saying, "Healthy is whatever I define as healthy."

Put mathematically: My truth > Biological truth.

If we can't agree on medical truth, how can we build consensus around far less clear (but equally important) matters such as policing, education, free speech, and justice? The answer is: we can't. Instead, discourse devolves into a battle between the critical theory tribe and their archrivals: conspiracy theorists.

Conspiracy Theories
QAnon

A friend of mine texted me out of the blue with a link to an Instagram profile. She asked, "Do you know who this is?"

The link took me to a Christian mommy blogger trafficking in all the normal social media tropes: Bible verses in cursive script, family photos carefully staged to look authentic, complaining about parenting, bragging about parenting, and of course, a little dabbling in multi-level marketing.

I responded, "Yeah, I've heard of her."

A second link popped up on our thread. "Well, did you see this?"

It was an image from the mommy blogger's Instagram feed reading, "Save the children." At first, I didn't think it was strange. It was probably a new cause I hadn't heard about.

But then I read the post's caption. The mommy blogger explained that there's a vast network of tunnels under Central Park in New York City. At the time, COVID tests were being administered in Central Park, but she explained this "COVID show" was staged to distract the public from what was happening underground: children were being trafficked through tunnels to feed the predatory sexual appetites of New York elites like politicians, actors, and journalists.

This was my first introduction to a conspiracy theory called QAnon, which grew out of dark-web social media sites like 4chan and has since become popular in some evangelical circles. Like most conspiracies, it's difficult to summarize because it has many forms. But Mark Sayers, who we had on our podcast, summed it up for me better than anyone else:

> QAnon is a rapidly growing global, cultural, and political movement that is centered around a crowd-sourced conspiracy theory.
>
> The group centers itself around the idea that the world is controlled and held back by a cabal of elite pedophiles. This group ranges from members of the Democrat party like the Clintons, to people in banking like the Rothschilds, to the Royals, to the Vatican, to members of Wall Street, and celebrities.
>
> This evil, nefarious force in the world is being pushed back essentially by President Trump, who is being supported by various patriots, including the military and military intelligence.
>
> We are in a moment which is moving toward what's called "the Storm," which is a reckoning, a judgment day, for this global cabal of elites. This might be imprisonment or death and will lead to a Golden Age of America.
>
> And all of this has been sparked by an internet poster named "Q," who gives "drops" of insight and knowledge from the Trump White House or military intelligence. He is telegraphing what to expect in this grand narrative.[5]

In the aftermath of the 2020 election, QAnon became much more visible to everyday people. Supporters claimed not only that the election was stolen from Trump but also that the coming storm would set things right.[6] This explains why QAnon shaman Jake Angeli—of Viking-helm, fur-wearing, chest-tattooed, and face-painted fame—helped lead the January 6 riot at the Capitol.

Many Christians—on both the right and the left—were surprised to see *many* Christian posters among the rioters, right alongside the ones supporting Q. I was not surprised.

In the months leading up to the election, I heard more and more stories of Christian family members and friends who were being sucked into the conspiracy theory. I met with concerned parents, children, and siblings.

I tried my best to pastor them. I gave them tips on how to charitably listen and persuade them with indisputable, objective evidence. *Not one person was able to persuade a loved one to leave Q behind.*

They all told me alarmingly similar stories. Q supporters wrote off all evidence that contradicted their narrative—be it photos, videos, interviews, research, history, or journalism—as fabrications from the MSM (mainstream media).[7] They said that anyone who disagreed with them was part of the "sheeple"—people brainwashed by media and the academy.

In other words, there is no truth but the truth of QAnon. The only valid authority on truth is Q and the Q community. In other words, the truth is subjective. Objective, external realities from outside the tribe are invalid. Unfortunately, an entirely subjective truth, rooted only in the opinions of the tribe, not only makes culture wars inevitable, it makes them unresolvable.

COVID Vaccines and Absolute Certainty

A friend of mine, Jason, met up for dinner with one of his longtime friends, Brad. They hadn't seen each other for quite some time because of the pandemic. And the conversation was great!

Until it got weird.

Brad explained to Jason, "I will *never* get the COVID vaccine. It turns people into genetically modified organisms."

Jason, who happens to have a PhD in genetics, explained that while there might be some legitimate reasons to wait on a vaccine, Brad's information was not correct. Because Jason's specialty was, in fact, genetically modified organisms, he knew—beyond a shadow of a doubt—that a vaccine could not turn a human into a GMO.

Did Jason's evidence change Brad's mind? No.

Brad responded, "You're just drinking the Kool-Aid. That's what *they* taught you to believe in school. It's all a lie."

> ### AN ENTIRELY SUBJECTIVE TRUTH, ROOTED ONLY IN THE OPINIONS OF THE TRIBE, NOT ONLY MAKES CULTURE WARS INEVITABLE, IT MAKES THEM UNRESOLVABLE.

When Jason shared this story with me, I thought about a podcast interview we did with Greg Locke, one of the most visible anti-vaccine pastors in the country. The interview was part of a series in which we talked to people we strongly disagreed with as a way of modeling civil discourse. After we debated the merits of vaccines, I asked him a question: "On a scale of one to ten, with one being totally uncertain and ten being absolutely certain, how certain are you that you're right about vaccines?"

He responded, "I'm twenty. I'm way past ten. I'm ten to the tenth power, bro."

I asked him whether I could present him with any evidence that would change his mind. He doubled down. "No. I've studied it well. I know a lot of people. No, there's no way."[8]

His answer made one thing clear: Greg wasn't open to the truth.

People who are open to the truth rarely give anything a ten out of ten on the certainty scale, and they're always willing to hear contrary evidence. This is because they know that their opinions and preferences don't make something objectively true. There is an objective world outside of their subjective experiences, and because they want to know the truth, they allow the givens of that objective world to correct their subjective understanding. Greg Locke's overconfidence in his *personal* truth closed his mind to *objective* truth.

Of course, Greg isn't alone. Our world is being swamped by "lowercase t" truths, which are rooted in subjective opinion, characterized by absolute certainty, and closed to outside evidence. This is precisely why advocates of these tribal truths rarely rely on reasoned persuasion. Instead, they use misinformation, propaganda, and if necessary, verbal force to win.

Anyone pedaling "*my* truth"—whether they're a critical theorist or a conspiracy theorist—is dealing in a dangerous form of intellectual tribalism that inevitably leads to the pitched culture wars tearing our nation and churches apart.

Without Truth There Is Only Coercion

America has always been a pluralistic society. Different groups have sought to prove their vision of the common good and persuade others in the public square. But when a culture ceases to believe in shared "capital T" truth, persuasion is impossible. When truth is a matter of personal taste, preference reigns, not reason. Who are you, after all, to say that vanilla is better than caramel, or that QAnon is better than fat studies?

In the absence of persuasion, there's only power. Whichever group controls academia, media, businesses, and our political institutions wins. Whichever group is in the majority is right.

Those who break with their tribe's orthodoxy in the name of "capital T" truth are coerced back into alignment or ousted, because their countervailing perspective jeopardizes the tribe's power.

The church has its own broken history of choosing the tools of power over persuasion (such as the Spanish Inquisition and Puritan witch hunts). Choosing this kind of coercion over persuasion is always demonic.

Consider the difference between demonic possession and the indwelling of the Holy Spirit. Demons violently control their subjects' bodies and minds.[9] The Spirit, however, indwells people as an empowering, guiding presence.[10] The Spirit can be resisted, but demons broker no resistance.[11] The Spirit persuades. The demonic coerces.

But this is beside the *main* point.

The main point is that the Bible claims to tell a "capital T" true story, which explains universal truths about God, humanity, good, evil, and the trajectory of the world.

When Jesus stood trial before Pontius Pilate, the Roman governor cynically asked Jesus, "What is truth?"[12] Pilate would fit well into the relativistic, tribal microcosm of twenty-first-century America. And this is precisely why he could not understand Jesus.

Jesus was not a cynic. He believed in Universal Truth and taught that *this* "truth will set you free."[13] He understood that lies chain you. They are tools of demonic coercion, used to bind you, dehumanize you, and enslave you to corrosive thought patterns that fill you with shame, anxiety, and sadness. Lies construct systems that deconstruct the common good, amplify division, and promote violence.

The apostle Paul warned Christians in Colossae, "See to it that no one takes you captive through hollow and deceptive philosophy, which depends on human tradition … rather than on Christ."[14] This was a command for their good, and it is a word we *desperately* need today.

As our tribalized society peddles a menagerie of personal truths, the church should remain a bastion of Universal Truth. We should resist the "theories" deconstructing the lives and chaining the minds of people by persuasively living out beautiful truth in community.

We should link arms with those who embrace healthy uncertainty and allow objective reality to correct their thinking precisely because we know the one who *made* reality. Following the truth, whatever twists and turns it may take, will ultimately only lead us to him.

Discussion and Reflection Questions

1. Read Colossians 2:8. What are some of the tribal theories and philosophies that you see taking other people captive?

2. What tribal theories and philosophies do you find most tempting personally?

3. Jesus claims to have access to truth with a capital "T." Where are you tempted to mistrust Jesus and choose your tribe's truth over Jesus's truth?

Chapter 9

WHY YOUR COMMUNITY IS TRIBAL

If you talk with a baby boomer who grew up in small-town America, he will tell you stories about knowing his neighbors, sharing potluck meals, and leaving doors unlocked. But if you go to those same communities today and pull up a seat at the local bar (if it's still there), you're likely to hear a different story. You'll hear about young people leaving and never coming back, family members dying after opioid overdoses, the elderly shrinking away into depressed isolation, and an overwhelming sense that you can't trust your neighbors anymore.

As one man told Tim Carney, the author of *Alienated America*, "I got a loaded .22 right by my door. I don't trust nobody in my apartment complex."[1]

The doors are locked now.

I don't write this out of nostalgia for the past. It's not hard to point out the dark side of small towns in the '50s and '60s as well. I write it because it's a microcosm of our cultural moment. In America, social trust is eroding at a rapid rate. What else should we expect when an entire nation was isolated by a pandemic, polarized by contested elections, and alienated from one another by partisan news outlets and nefarious social media algorithms?

Where trust withers, tribalism flourishes. For the simple reason that it's easier to disdain and judge those you don't know or trust. A deficit of social capital creates a surplus of hatred and division.

Social capital is a fancy term used by sociologists to describe something simple: How connected you are to other people. How many friendships, partnerships, obligations, relationships, communities, or groups you belong in. Social capital is *wealth in relationships*.

As it turns out, social capital is more important to your overall well-being than the ordinary kind of capital: money. Studies show that those who are wealthy in relationships experience the greatest levels of happiness, regardless of their bank accounts. The communities with the highest number of shared institutions (places where we find community like churches, bowling leagues, PTAs, and volunteer societies) are *also* the communities where children are most likely to rise out of poverty and people are least likely to experience depression, anxiety, crime, and drug and alcohol abuse.

None of this should surprise Christians.

The first thing God called "not good" wasn't sin. It was Adam's isolation.[2] You were designed by God to flourish in a robust, trusting, generous, self-giving network of relationships. Without it, you wither.

The Decline of Bowling and the Rise of Depression

The year 2019 saw some of the highest rates of anxiety and depression ever recorded.[3] Not to be beat, 2020 saw some of those numbers triple, and they've only increased since then.[4] Today, anyone with eyes and an ounce of empathy can see that isolation is at an all-time high and trust is at an all-time low.

Unfortunately, we've been on this trajectory for quite a while.

Once upon a time, Americans joined bowling leagues for camaraderie, but today we bowl alone. Once upon a time, Americans attended church alongside neighbors, but today more churches are shuttering their doors than ever before. Once upon a time, Americans lived with or near extended family, but today more than a quarter of the population lives alone.[5]

> **You were designed by God to flourish in a robust, trusting, generous, self-giving network of relationships. Without it, you wither.**

The trends toward isolation began before 2020, but the nationwide quarantine only made things worse. It exiled white-collar workers to a purgatory of remote work, moved more of life online, pressed pause on local gatherings, and alienated more Americans.

You've probably experienced the pain personally. As your local connections erode, so does your sense of belonging. As your sense of belonging decreases, so does your sense of trust in local leaders and friends. As your sense of local trust evaporates, you find yourself more open to tribalized experts or leaders with national platforms whose theories promise to explain *and* resolve the problems plaguing society.

Just ask yourself: Do you feel connected, integrated, and known in your local community? Do you feel less connected? Do you spend time with friends and family multiple times per week *outside* of work? Do you have a church, club, or group that you socialize with at least once a week? Do you spend more of your life online today than you did five years ago? Do you trust local people less? Do you trust your pastor or church less? Do you find yourself drawn to theories explaining society's problems?

Your answers to those questions will tell you how socially wealthy you are. They may also prove my point: you're living through the Great Depression of social capital, and it's miserable.

The Richest Neighborhoods in America

Of course, not all communities are poor in social capital. Some areas still have flourishing informal and formal associations: hot yoga classes, business networking clubs, charity boards, HOAs, restaurants, and country clubs.

But these associations all share one thing in common: you need monetary wealth to participate in them.

More and more college-educated Americans are moving into wealthier suburbs where the high cost of entry keeps middle America *outside*. This is not for nefarious reasons: They want the best schools and sidewalks for their kids. They want quick and easy access to amenities.[6]

As Carney showed in *Alienated America*, the wealthiest of these communities are increasingly coastal, white, liberal, college educated, and irreligious. Their constituents, though concerned for those in need, often have a difficult time understanding the situation of their poorer counterparts elsewhere.[7]

People who work two jobs don't have time for PTAs. They can't afford hot yoga or the country club. They live in apartments or neighborhoods populated mostly by renters—so there's no neighborhood association. Instead, there's lots of transience and little opportunity to build trust.

As you can imagine, this socioeconomic separation leads to tremendous misunderstanding.

Let me paint in broad brushstrokes: Wealthy, mostly white members of elite communities often misrepresent poorer, rural whites as uneducated, backwater simpletons whose support of Donald Trump was a dog whistle for covert racism. They're nostalgic for a racist past and hold our country behind. The wealthy elite's position in academia, the corporate managerial class, and America's top tech and media organizations allows them to mainstream their views publicly.

Rural white communities, where poverty is growing every year, feel this condescension palpably and respond in kind. They voted for Trump because they wanted to go back to a day when their towns were lively and their relationships were thick, not because they're racists. They resent the ways coastal elites portray them in the media—which explains their mistrust of media—but feel hopeless about changing anything. They have almost *no* institutional power in an increasingly globalized world, and they will throw their support behind anyone who promises to give them a voice.

Neither side knows each other. Their mutual mistrust is oxygen for the fire of tribalism and misunderstanding.

This picture fits well with the findings from a recent More in Common study, which found that the most tribalized wings of our society are *majority white*. America's culture wars are being waged by two wildly opposed white communities, battling for their visions of the future. Everyone else, including much of the middle class and most people of color, are left in the middle, exhausted.

And all of this was predicted two hundred years ago by Alexis de Tocqueville.

When the World Becomes a Stranger

The American Revolution sparked other democratic revolutions throughout the world, but none was more bloody or self-defeating than the French Revolution. After several failed iterations, numerous wars, and thousands of guillotined bodies, it ended in the rise of an autocrat named Napoléon Bonaparte—whose own life was a roller coaster of glory, blood, and failure.

In the aftermath, a Frenchman named Alexis de Tocqueville decided to travel around America in order to understand why democracy succeeded there but failed in France.

His conclusion was that Americans consistently formed local associations to work for the common good. They did not rely on an aristocracy or on the government. But Alexis warned that all of this could change. He imagined a future dystopia where Americans isolated themselves from one another:

> Each of them, withdrawn and apart, is like a stranger to the destiny of all the others: his children and his particular friends form the whole human species for him; as for dwelling with his fellow citizens, he is beside them, but he does not see them; he touches them and does not feel them; he exists only in himself and for himself alone, and if a family still remains for him, one can at least say that he no longer has a native country.[8]

He was prophetic. His words almost perfectly described America *today*.

With the exception of our families, coworkers, and closest friends, our fellow citizens have become strangers. Our lack of proximity to people whose lives are wildly different from our own makes us insensitive to their plights. Vehicles allowed us to segregate socioeconomically into suburbs and gated communities. The few places where we once rubbed shoulders with those whose economic circumstances were different from our own are disappearing.

Without these shared spaces, all you have are the media proxies of our neighbors. You only know the caricatures presented to you by the news or on social media. And like all caricatures, they are clownish, revealing more about the artist than the subject. But you forget this, beginning to hate the clown you don't know, defining yourself by a tribe that looks and thinks like you and, perhaps most importantly, *is not like them.*

Before Tocqueville's nightmare becomes a complete reality, it is imperative that we work together to rebuild social trust. And as it turns out, Jesus founded the one institution that does this superlatively: *the church.*

The Only Get-Rich-Quick Scheme That Works

No localized association has been more important in American history than the church. And empirically speaking, this is a good thing. Religious people are happier, more connected, and less likely to commit crimes or suffer from mental illness. During the COVID pandemic, one study found that every American demographic experienced a decline in mental well-being except for one: those who attended church on a weekly basis.

This is because Jesus is the source of life and true happiness. Of course, I'm not naive enough to believe that *every* churchgoer is living happily. But I do believe that regular church attenders experience things that are fundamental to human well-being: community, belonging, and connection.

The church also has one thing going that elite associations of the wealthy do not have: *it's free.*

Unlike country clubs and gated neighborhoods, the church welcomes people from every socioeconomic bracket and prides itself especially on helping those most in need.

I experience this constantly as a pastor. In one day, I can have breakfast with a CEO, lunch with an ex-drug addict, happy hour with a middle manager, and dinner with a guy on parole. In a Bible study, I'll see a single mom struggling to make it sitting alongside a retiree living off a 401(k)—both learning from each other and serving each other! I've led small groups with college dropouts and PhDs. When our elders gather, I see people of different races, with different family backgrounds and wildly different vocations.

None of this is remarkable. It's just the church.

Unfortunately, studies show that churches are disappearing in two places: elite liberal enclaves and impoverished rural communities. The wealthy have the means to create alternative spaces for community and belonging, but the impoverished just lose it all.

Here's my hot take: planting more churches in socially poor neighborhoods will do more to lift people out of poverty than any government program or charity organization possibly could. I'm not against those other types of aid; I'm just *for* fundamental fixes. And humans are fundamentally made for thick relationships and deep trust.

Rebuilding Trust through the Church

The other major benefit of a (healthy) church is that it de-tribalizes people. Now, I should be clear: I'm not talking about churches that have been politically co-opted by the right or the left. Those are easy to spot. One has an American flag out front. The other has a rainbow flag.

But churches that fly the (figurative) Jesus flag above all else will draw people from every race, class, and political stripe.[9] These churches will create proximity between diverse people that happens nowhere else. And this enables what sociologists call "crosscutting relationships."

These are relationships that cut across socioeconomic, racial, and political boundaries, thereby significantly moderating tribalism.

Lest you think I'm a hopeless idealist, I'm not suggesting that conservatives will cease to be conservative or vice versa. But I do believe that if a liberal spends an hour every week with a conservative, he will be slower to believe clownish stereotypes about conservatives.

The apostle Paul was an expert at building congregations with crosscutting relationships, so it's no surprise that the advice he gave to the church in Rome applies to us also:

"For by the grace given me I say to every one of you: Do not think of yourself more highly than you ought.... In Christ we, though many, form one body, and each member belongs to all the others."[10]

It's true. If you want to be in a community full of diverse, cross-cutting relationships, you'll need to think less of yourself and more of others. You'll need to remember that the Democrat sitting across from you is part of the same body. Be thankful for her. Learn from her. Love her. As Paul wrote later in the same letter, "Accept each other just as Christ has accepted you."[11]

> IF YOU WANT TO BE IN A COMMUNITY FULL OF DIVERSE, CROSSCUTTING RELATIONSHIPS, YOU'LL NEED TO THINK LESS OF YOURSELF AND MORE OF OTHERS.

I believe that there is nothing more glorifying to Jesus and attractive to the outside world than a church that's rich in social capital, rich in crosscutting relationships, rich in acceptance, and rich in sacrificial love for the *other* tribe.

Discussion and Reflection Questions

1. Do you have any *close* crosscutting relationships (i.e., a friendship with someone from a different race, political party, education level, or socioeconomic bracket)? If so, what do you appreciate about that friendship? If not, what prevents you from developing those relationships?

2. Social trust is at an all-time low. How do you see and experience the lack of social trust in your community?

3. What can you do to help the church catalyze more crosscutting relationships in your community? How would that glorify Jesus?

Part Three

How to Leave Tribalism Behind

Do you want to put an end to tribalism in your community?

In parts 1 and 2, you saw how tribalism is destroying our society. There's nothing the devil wants more than division and hatred. But Jesus offers another way. *There is hope.* So it's time to get practical and look at seven ways Jesus calls us to resist tribalism.

In part 3, you'll learn how Jesus is calling you into God's presence (chapter 10) so that you can show radical generosity and kindness (chapter 11), pledge your allegiance to him and not a political party (chapter 12), admit when you're wrong (chapter 13), cross tribal lines (chapter 14), listen to diverse voices (chapter 15), and join an inclusive tribe (chapter 16).

It is our prayer that every chapter will give you one practical step you can take into your everyday life to choose the truth of Jesus over the lies of tribalism. We understand that this is a lifelong process, not a onetime decision. If you want to continue that journey, scan the QR code below to receive access to our weekly email newsletter and podcast.

Chapter 10

You Journey toward Eden

In an iconic scene from the 1991 film *Grand Canyon*, a tow truck driver (Danny Glover) comes to the aid of a stranded motorist (Kevin Kline) in a rough part of town. A gang has happened upon the broken-down car and is harassing the motorist when the tow service arrives.

After hitching the car to the back of his truck, Glover's character pulls the gang leader aside and politely asks him to let them leave. He explains that this isn't the way it's supposed to be. He's supposed to be able to do his job without being forced to negotiate with a gang. The driver of the car is supposed to be able to wait safely until help arrives. "Everything is supposed to be different than what it is."[1]

If you're looking for a slogan we can all rally around, maybe that's it. In a polarized world where people don't agree on much, it seems we can all agree with at least one thing: something is wrong with our world.

The question we argue over is this: Why is the world *not* the way it's supposed to be? Artists, protestors, and politicians all have their answers. What's yours?

Listen to the Artists ...

> I've got a God-shaped hole that's infected.
> And I'm petrified of being alone now. It's pathetic,
>   I know ...
> And if I believe you will that make it stop?
> If I told you I need you is that what you want?
> And I'm broken and bleeding and begging for help.
> And I'm asking you, Jesus, show yourself.[2]

These aren't lyrics from a worship song. They're the words of a self-identified atheist, Matthew Healy, in his song "If I Believe You." And other artists echo this theme: listen to Coldplay's "Broken," Sam Smith's "Pray," not to mention countless songs by Radiohead.

Today's singer-songwriter looks at the emptiness inside every person and says, "Maybe that's the problem? Maybe that's what's wrong with the world?"

Listen to the Protestors ...

But what if the singer-songwriters have it wrong? What if the real problem isn't inside your heart but outside, in the world? What if your problems come from social structures, social inequities, or social failures? What if all your problems are issues of injustice?

People on both sides of the political aisle attend rallies blaming the world's problems on social ills. We need only think about the protests after George Floyd's murder, the chants of "Build the wall," athletes taking a knee, the "Stop the Steal" rally that led to an attack on the Capitol, and corporate diversity seminars designed to cure inequity and racism. Protests point to a deep truth: something is wrong *out there*.

Nothing is the way it is supposed to be. You see that in your personal life. You see it in the systems and structures of your world. Maybe the biggest problem is simply that no one knows how to fix it.

The Bible's Cure for What Ails Us

The Bible explains why the world is broken, and it reveals the only thing that can fix it.

The story begins with human beings living with God in Eden, which is the Hebrew word for "Delight." The problem comes when those first humans rebel, get exiled from the Garden of Delight and banished from God's presence. Since then, the land of delight has felt far from present reality. But humans never stopped longing to return.

Your desire for a better world is a longing to return to Eden. You want to get back to the way the world was before human evil defiled it.

WHY IS THE WORLD NOT THE WAY IT'S SUPPOSED TO BE? ARTISTS, PROTESTORS, AND POLITICIANS ALL HAVE THEIR ANSWERS. WHAT'S YOURS?

When Adam and Eve were banished from Eden, God placed two armed cherubim on the *east* side of the garden so they couldn't return. After Cain killed his brother Abel, he left God's presence and settled *east* of Eden.[3] In Genesis, the further east you travel, the further from God you get.

The Bible says that *you* live east of Eden too.

Deep in your consciousness, you still remember the Garden of Delight. You *know* you were made for a world of love, justice, and mercy. And therefore, you feel dissatisfied with the world as it is. You're too far east. You want to return.

What Are You Running From?

Ben Schlappig, one of the world's greatest travel hackers, shared his experiences exploring the world for free in an interview with *Rolling Stone*. He traveled over 400,000 miles in forty-three weeks, flying first class the whole way.

Why does a person crisscross the Pacific Ocean six times in one trip, spending days at a time on airplanes and in airports? What's attractive about not having a home?

What's Ben running from?

When he was three years old, his fourteen-year-old brother, Marc, died in a boating accident. "Marc had been like a father to Ben," their mother told the magazine. "He was everything."[4]

Ben was inconsolable, so much so that his preschool asked his mom not to bring him back. The teachers couldn't get him to stop screaming. His only solace came when his mom took him to the airport and they watched planes take off and land. Maybe he imagined one of those planes would help him escape his pain?

His friend Nick Dierman thinks Ben is trying to escape the challenges of life.

If that's where the urge to run started, how's it going now?

Ben told the magazine that he wants to settle down some day. "You see a whole family, 20 people, picking up someone at the airport," he said. "People with signs, people with balloons, with flowers. There's something beautiful about that."

But he's not ready to stop yet. "The world is so big, I can keep running," Ben said. After a long pause, he continued, "I want what I can't have. There's nothing gratifying about that. It's crazy, and it's fucked up. I'd still like to think I'm a reasonably happy person." He grinned. "Despite all that."[5]

No one has to tell Ben that this world isn't the way it's supposed to be. Your fourteen-year-old brother isn't supposed to die. The pain isn't supposed to be so deep. Happiness and healing aren't supposed to be so elusive.

Ben is looking for Eden. He wants what he cannot have. Isn't that true of us also?

C. S. Lewis wrote:

> A man's physical hunger does not prove that man will get any bread; he may die of starvation on a raft in the Atlantic. But surely a man's hunger does prove that he comes of a race which repairs its body by eating and inhabits a world where edible substances exist. In the same way, though I do not believe that my desire for Paradise proves that I shall enjoy it, I think it a pretty good indication that such a thing exists and that some men will.[6]

We were made to live in relationship with God. Ever since sin ruptured our Eden, we've been trying to get back home.

Why do we join tribes? Because we long for the safe, loving, and supporting community that's found in Eden.

Why is there so much anger? Because east of Eden, we're searching for something to give our allegiance to while refusing the one who makes Eden a delight.

Why do we feel compelled to work for justice toward the vulnerable? Because we remember Eden and want to relieve suffering in the present world.

Why have politics become the new religion for so many? Because we desperately long for the ordered, just, and united society that God established in Eden.

Do you feel a longing for Eden in your heart? Do you feel a longing for the world to be right? I think we all do. And after the last few years, we all feel that longing more palpably than ever before. I think of my mom—whom I never remember making New Year's resolutions—coming to the end of 2020 and confiding in me that she hoped to somehow make 2021 better.

She put into words what a lot of people felt. And although she wasn't thinking about Genesis, I think what she really hoped for was to get back to Eden.

The Way Back to Eden

There's only one way back, and every politician, media mogul, activist, and friendly neighbor claims to have it. Every tribe offers some vision of Eden—the world as it should be. But all of these visions are a sham. You won't find your way back to Eden by reclaiming America's Christian heritage and making America great again, fixing every social inequity, or creating racial harmony. Your tribe's utopia may sound grand, but all utopian dreams share one thing in common: failure. Every tribe promises their own version of utopia, but not one can deliver on their promise.

The Bible starts with Adam and Eve walking with God in the Garden of Eden, and it ends with Jesus reigning over his kingdom fully established on earth. We live in the in-between—a time after humanity's fall yet before the eradication of sin. We live in the world as it's not supposed to be. We are broken people living a broken existence with a longing to return to a better place.

That better world—what the Bible calls the kingdom of God—isn't going to come through a social protest movement or a political candidate or a moral revolution. The truth is that your tribe isn't up to the challenge. Only God's king can bring God's kingdom.

Everyone wants the kingdom without the king because they want the kingdom on their own terms. But the king is the only way back to Eden. If you reject the king, then things will never be the way they are supposed to be.

The tabernacle and the temple reminded the Israelites that the only path back to Eden is past deadly cherubim wielding swords. This is why they sewed cherubim into the fabric of the curtains between the place where God dwelt and humans dwelt.

EVERYONE WANTS THE KINGDOM WITHOUT THE KING BECAUSE THEY WANT THE KINGDOM ON THEIR OWN TERMS.

To get back to Eden, to get back to God, someone had to pass under the sword. Jesus made a way for us. He experienced death so that we can have life. He gave up his heavenly home to make an eternal home for us. He was cut off from his father so we could have a family.

Everyone wants to get back to Eden. Only Jesus offers us a path back. It's a road less traveled. It's the journey of receiving forgiveness. It's the way of unearned grace. It's the trail cut by a king who loved his enemies, even unto death.

To walk on that path is to have your broken heart restored. To walk on that road is to have reality turned upside down. Enemies become friends. The unforgivable forgiven. The undeserving extended grace. This is the only way to make what's broken right again.

The utopian promises of committed tribalists can never fix the world. They only entrench the problem by repeating the cycle of anger, violence, and hatred. Only Jesus breaks that cycle by dying for those who hate him. Only Jesus's death and resurrection can take us west once more, to the Garden of Delight where everything is as it should be.

Discussion and Reflection Questions

1. How does tribalism make your life "not the way it's supposed to be"?

2. How does tribalism make you feel homeless and out of place in relationships?

3. Jesus died and rose again to welcome us back home with God. When you think about resurrected life, how will it be different from the present?

Chapter 11

You Show Generosity and Kindness

Imagine you are one of the many Americans living under crushing debt with little hope of escape. Now imagine you receive a letter explaining that *all* your debt was forgiven. School loans? Paid off. Mortgage? Erased. Credit card bill? Abolished.

Something like this happened every fifty years in ancient Israel. It was called "the Jubilee." A day of liberation. Debts forgiven. Indentured servants released. Mortgaged property returned. It happened on the annual Day of Atonement—meaning that once every fifty years everyone's moral and financial debts were forgiven *on the same day*. Scholars debate whether Israel actually practiced the Jubilee, but no one doubts that it expressed the heart and will of God. It's not hard to imagine the *jubilation* that would follow: all debts—material and spiritual—paid in full.

When a poor construction worker named Jesus of Nazareth sat down in his hometown's synagogue to teach the Scripture, he surprised everyone by choosing a strange passage. He didn't teach on the life of Abraham or King David. He didn't exposit one of Daniel's apocalyptic visions. He chose a passage about the Jubilee:

Unrolling it, he found the place where it is written:

"The Spirit of the Lord is on me,
    because he has anointed me
    to proclaim good news to the poor.
He has sent me to proclaim freedom for the
    prisoners
    and recovery of sight for the blind,
to set the oppressed free,
    to proclaim the year of the Lord's favor."

Then he rolled up the scroll, gave it back to the attendant and sat down. The eyes of everyone in the synagogue were fastened on him. He began by saying to them, "Today this scripture is fulfilled in your hearing."[1]

Jesus told the shocked crowd that *he* was the Jubilee to end all Jubilees. He was bringing the ultimate day of liberation from all debts—even the debt of judgment we owed God for choosing evil. Of course, this begs a question, "How *did* Jesus forgive my debt?"

The answer is a Roman cross. Jesus died in your place so he could send you a letter that says, "Your debts have been paid." And not just you. Jesus offers the gift of forgiveness to people of every political tribe, ethnicity, gender, economic status, and sexual orientation. To accept that gift, you do not need to check off any identity boxes. You only need to confess your sin and turn from it to God.

Jesus's singular act of debt cancellation strikes a blow against tribalism because it tears down the "dividing wall of hostility" that separates human communities, thereby establishing a "new humanity" united in Jesus.[2] How? By flattening the differences between us in two ways:

1. Jesus's undeserved gift strips us of everything we use to exalt ourselves: our political identity, ethnic identity, economic identity, and cultural identity. To receive his gift, you must first acknowledge that none of these things make you right with God. The truth is that you are a broken, rebellious, corrupt insurrectionist against God's kingdom. None of your achievements or identities can pay off your debt. This means you are no better (and no different) than anyone else. There can be no tribal superiority at the foot of the cross. We are *all* sinners.

2. Jesus's free gift is precisely what exalts you. The apostle Paul wrote, "For you know the grace of our Lord Jesus Christ, that though he was rich, yet for your sake he became poor, so that you through his poverty might become rich."[3] Not only has our debt been paid by the sacrifice of Christ, but through faith we're given his wealth. The wealth Paul was speaking about is the promise of a glorious future— the resurrection—which we begin to experience

through transformation in the present. Your tribe is
not what makes you glorious. Jesus is the one who
gives you eternal value, glory, and worth.

With so much in common, how can we be divided? Why would
unworthy recipients of God's grace cling to worldly, temporal forms
of superiority?

Jesus's jubilant, generous, self-sacrificial debt cancellation is the
greatest known weapon against tribalism and division.

WITH SO MUCH IN COMMON, HOW CAN WE BE DIVIDED?

When you receive your letter from Jesus, "Every debt is paid
off," it liberates you from tribal pride and frees you to be equally
generous so that you can retell the Jubilee story in your community.

If you do, don't be surprised when the walls of division tumble
down.

A Modern Jubilee

In 2019, many people in our city suffered under the burden of
substantial medical debt, which is one of the leading causes of bank-
ruptcy in our state. Here, about half of all debt collection is related
to unpaid medical expenses. Those burdened by this debt receive
threatening letters and experience the embarrassment of collection
agencies hounding family and friends. Their credit ratings plummet.
Finding housing becomes difficult.

Because Jesus set our church free from our spiritual debt, our
church felt called to set others free.

That's why we teamed up with an organization called RIP Medical Debt to pay off the medical debt of people making less than twice the poverty rate (under $51,500 per year for a family of four).[4] Because their medical debt is unlikely to be paid, collection agencies are willing to sell it for one penny on the dollar. This means that $1 can buy $100 of medical debt, and $100 can buy $10,000.

We pitched the idea to our church, with the (perhaps unattainable) goal of paying off the medical debt of every person in our city and county. As it turns out, that goal was far too low. Our church gave $430,000 to forgive $43 million of medical debt. Their generosity forgave the medical debt of *thirty-one counties* in Missouri.

All the beneficiaries received a letter informing them that their medical debt was forgiven in the name of Jesus. Christians and atheists received letters. Straight people and gay people received letters. Men and women received letters. Black, white, Latino, and Asian people received letters.

Generosity in the name of Jesus knows no tribal borders.

What happened next was astonishing: local tribalism began to crumble. Letters, emails, and phone calls flooded in from people asking, "Why did you do this? I'm not a Christian. I don't deserve this."

We responded to them all in the same way, "Neither do we."

People from every imaginable background—and not just those whose debts were paid—began to appear in church, moved by our generosity to explore the far greater generosity of Jesus. I remember grabbing lunch with an atheist who once was loudly anti-Christian. We were the "them" he loved to attack. But at lunch, he told me that seeing what we did eroded his hatred. It made him interested in Jesus for the first time in a long time.

And the same thing happens whenever we, as a church, show generosity. One Christmas, we gave to provide electric lights to impoverished people in central Africa. One Easter, we raised $675,000 to cancel the utility debt of every family in our city at risk of utility disconnection.

Every time, the response to generosity is similar: walls fall. The love and beauty of Jesus bring our city together. And not just that. Generosity unites our church. It doesn't matter whether you're on the left or the right—we all agree that sharing a small fraction of the generosity we've received from Jesus is a good thing.

Tribalism simply cannot withstand the weight of self-sacrificial generosity. It always breaks under the pressure of a gift freely given. Of course, financial generosity is not the only variety of generosity. So what are the other forms we can apply to combating tribalism?

Time, Encouragement, and Kindness

Tribalists are often known more by what they're *against* than what they're *for*. My friend and fellow pastor-podcaster Brad Edwards calls this an "anti-vision."[5] There's no vision for what you want to *build*, just a vision for what you seek to *destroy*. The problem is that anti-visions die once they've devoured their enemies, leaving only rubble behind.

Jesus did not establish the church with an anti-vision. He established it with a constructive vision.

First and foremost, we're kingdom builders. This means that, as a Christian, you should be known more by what you're *for* than what you're *against*. And self-sacrificial generosity is the best tool for this building project.

> ## TRIBALISM SIMPLY CANNOT WITHSTAND THE WEIGHT OF SELF-SACRIFICIAL GENEROSITY.

If you want to be known by what you're for, be generous with your time, encouragement, and kindness:

◊ **Giving Time**

A church that serves is a church that's *for* something.

Our church's members spread throughout the city to make a difference in the lives of hurting people. If you're an at-risk high school student, you shouldn't be surprised if a member of The Crossing is the first to offer tutoring and a meal. If you're a refugee moving to Columbia, there's a good chance one of your first contacts will be someone who's a part of The Crossing. If you're homeless and are working to rebuild your life, you shouldn't be surprised if you start alongside someone connected to The Crossing. If you're a woman fleeing domestic abuse with your family, there's a good chance you'll experience the love of Jesus from one of our members at a local shelter.

James warned, "If one of you says to them, 'Go in peace; keep warm and well fed,' but does nothing about their physical needs, what good is it?"[6] If the church is known as a place that *speaks* peace but does not *build* it, then who's surprised when no one is convinced? A church that crosses tribal lines to love everyone in word and deed is a church empowered by God's spirit to topple tribalism.

If you're not actively serving somewhere, how will people know that you're *for* anything bigger than your tribe?

◊ **Giving Public Encouragement**

A church that shows encouragement is a church that's *for* something.

Nowhere is public encouragement more important today than on social media. I know this firsthand. When I rejoined Twitter after a decade-long hiatus, it immediately appealed to my worst desires. I found myself seeking out people I could disagree with, zeroing in on what they got wrong, and then dunking on them. *I was becoming known for what I was against.*

And then someone returned the favor. It was a wake-up call, because when I was the one critiqued, intentionally misunderstood, and maligned, I easily saw how much it hurt. I also saw how *un*winsome it was. No one trusts a troll. I suddenly realized that I was doing unto others exactly what I didn't want done unto me. So I reached out to every person I'd dunked on and apologized. After that, I made a new rule: only use comments and likes to encourage people. Seek out what is true and good and celebrate *that*. Ignore the rest.

The apostle Paul advised, "Whatever is true, whatever is noble, whatever is right, whatever is pure, whatever is lovely, whatever is admirable—if anything is excellent or praiseworthy—think about such things."[7] Today, public takedowns are the norm. Tribes do everything they can to protect their own and dunk on others. Shouldn't the church be known as the one institution that publicly offers love, not condemnation? Isn't that how Jesus treats us?

How do you need to change your demeanor on social media? How can you publicly encourage others?

◊ **Giving Kindness**

A church that shows kindness is a church that's *for* something.

When I became a Christian, I began to hear about something called "apologetics." That's a fancy word for "defending your faith." People told me that to be an effective "apologist," I needed to know arguments defending the existence of God and the truthfulness of the Bible. I quickly discovered that these required mighty philosophical powers that outstrip most mortals. So perhaps it's no surprise that I, like most Christians, felt out of my depth in the "defending my faith" department.

But I've got good news: hardly anyone I talk to these days asks *the kind of* questions apologists answer. Generally, people ask simple questions: *Is Jesus good? Can Jesus heal my broken life? Is his way of life loving? Does following him create beauty?* These questions are best answered with deeds, not words. And such deeds require something that, by God's grace, lies within every mortal's reach: *kindness.*

As our culture devolves into increasing outrage, unkindness, and vitriol, you should stand out as an alternative. You do this by responding to unkind words with charity: "Thanks for challenging me. I'll have to think more about it and see what I can learn." You do this by showing empathy to someone who is hurting: "I'd be hurting if I were you too. Can you tell me more about what you're feeling?" You do this by slowing down to help someone in need: "I don't have to be anywhere. How can I help?"

You should do this with non-Christians. And of course, you should do this with your Christian brothers and sisters. After all, Jesus said, "By this everyone will know that you are my disciples, if you love one another."[8]

Who can you give kindness to today?

What Will You Be Known For?

If you're known by what you're *for*, it will be difficult for tribalists to make you play their game. They won't know what to do with you because you won't fit their paradigm. If they label people "good" or "bad" based on their tribal association, then your refusal to participate—because you know that we're *all* broken before God—may infuriate them. They might write you off. They might accuse you of minimizing the urgency of the moment. They might claim you're against them. They might try to turn others against you.

But remember: they did this to Jesus too. And he didn't condemn them. Instead, he said, "Father, forgive them, for they do not know what they are doing."[9] He showed generosity and kindness in the face of violent hatred. We must do likewise because that is the final and greatest act of generosity we can offer—love toward those who persecute us.

It will shock onlookers. It might even shock the person attacking you. If they ask you why you show such love, remember this simple answer: *Jesus did it for me. Now I'm free to do it for others. Why don't you join me?*

Discussion and Reflection Questions

1. How have you seen kindness and generosity tear down walls between people?

2. How is God calling you to be generous to people in a different tribe? How can you give time, public encouragement, and kindness?

3. How does Jesus's generosity to you enable you to show generosity to others?

Chapter 12

You Pledge Allegiance to Jesus

In 2017, Tim Farron resigned from his position as the party leader of the United Kingdom's Liberal Democrats. He had, up until then, consistently voted for the liberalizing of the UK's marriage laws to expand the definition of marriage to include same-sex couples. Yet as a Christian, he believed the Bible taught that gay sex was a sin. This was not a perspective he shared publicly, but it leaked to the press. During the months leading up to his resignation, journalists and party members pressed him to change his personal view.[1]

Unlike most politicians who glibly change their views to improve their political prospects, Farron refused to be intellectually inauthentic. He explained why in his resignation speech: "I joined our party when I was 16. It is in my blood. I love our history, our people. I thoroughly love my party. So, imagine how proud I am to lead this party. And then imagine what would lead me to voluntarily relinquish that honor. In the words of Isaac Watts, it would have to be something 'so amazing, so divine, that it demands my heart, my life, my all.'" Farron continued, "To be a leader, particularly of a progressive liberal party in 2017, and to live as a committed Christian and to hold faithful to the Bible's teaching has felt impossible for me."[2]

Ultimately, when forced to pick between Jesus and his party, Farron chose Jesus. Try to put yourself in his shoes. Can you imagine what you would do if your life, reputation, future, and career all hung on that choice?

Who gets my highest allegiance: Jesus or my tribe? How would you answer that question today?

Becoming a Political Free Agent

Keith and I are recovering partisan tribalists. We both know what it's like to put politics and party *first*.

In 1994, Keith lived through the Republican Revolution (also known as the Gingrich Revolution), when Republicans took the House of Representatives for the first time in forty years. When Keith heard the news, he went outside, took his shirt off, and began running in circles cheering. And no, he wasn't drunk.

But he was intoxicated by hope. With Republicans in charge, *things would change.*

In 2008, I attended an Obama campaign rally on the University of Missouri's campus. I felt electrified by his message of care and provision for those in economic distress. When he won the election a month later, I didn't take my shirt off. But I definitely cheered.

I was intoxicated by hope. With a Democrat in charge, *things would change.*

We were not political free agents. We each truly believed that our party's platform was the path to a brighter future and that the other party would condemn America to a second dark age. Belonging to a political tribe was a heady, almost religious experience: camaraderie with like-minded friends, faith in the cause, and the condemnation of lost outsiders.

We loved it.

But then something happened to us: the teachings of Jesus.

Jesus Is Political, Not Partisan

Who would Jesus vote for? What do you think? A Republican? A Democrat? Maybe Jesus would write himself in? That's not a bad guess, but you'd be wrong.

Here's the correct answer: Jesus can't vote. He's not an American citizen.

I'm not trying to be coy. I'm making a serious point: Jesus wasn't a citizen of Rome or any commonwealth during his lifetime.

This has led some Christians throughout history to wrongly imagine that Jesus is apolitical. He's here to save souls, not society. But this hardly computes with what Jesus said about himself. He had a bad habit of talking about political entities, like "kingdoms." In fact, announcing "the gospel of *the kingdom*" seemed to be his favorite pastime.[3]

Kingdoms *are* political. He talked about other politically charged topics too, like money and taxation, sex and marriage, the treatment of wrongdoers and enemies, the proper orientation toward civil and military authorities—and the list goes on.

Jesus had a politic. You might wonder, what's a politic? Lee Camp, professor of theology and ethics at Lipscomb University, offered a helpful definition:

> [A politic is] an all-encompassing manner of communal life that grapples with all the questions the

classical art of politics has always asked: How do
we live together? How do we deal with offenses?
How do we deal with money? How do we deal with
enemies and violence? How do we arrange marriage
and families and social structures? How is authority mediated, employed, ordered? How do we
rightfully order passions and appetites? And much
more besides, but most especially add these: Where
is human history headed? What does it mean to
be human? And what does it look like to live in a
rightly ordered human community that engenders
flourishing, justice, and the peace of God?[4]

The tribes of the left and the right both offer answers to each of
these questions. And so does King Jesus. That's because he's political, but he's not partisan. In other words, Jesus doesn't support
the Democratic platform or the Republican platform. His vision
of God's kingdom on earth doesn't neatly fit into either tribal
ideology.

Jesus tells us to welcome immigrants *and* protect the unborn, to
pursue radical chastity *and* radical justice, to create order *and* create
art, to ensure the livelihoods of the poor *and* the wealthy, to share
our tables with the powerful *and* the powerless, to affirm our varied
ethnic identities *and* cling to what unites us.

JESUS DOESN'T SUPPORT THE DEMOCRATIC PLATFORM OR THE
REPUBLICAN PLATFORM. HIS VISION OF GOD'S KINGDOM ON
EARTH DOESN'T NEATLY FIT INTO EITHER TRIBAL IDEOLOGY.

Some of the things on that list fit both parties. Some just one. Some neither. That's why Jesus isn't a partisan. He has his own politic. *Remember: Jesus is not a citizen of the United States or any other country.* He is only a citizen of heaven. To be even more precise, he is the king over heaven. And as it turns out, heaven has its own unique politic.

What Is Heaven?

Throughout the Bible, "heaven" is never described as the place human souls go after death (true as that may be). Heaven is primarily understood as the place from which God rules and reigns over all creation.[5] Heaven is where Jesus is seated on a throne as king at the right hand of the Father.[6] Heaven is the place from which Jesus will return to earth as king.[7]

In other words, heaven is the throne room and command center of a king who's set himself over every caesar, emperor, king, dictator, prime minister, and president. Conceptually, heaven is closer to the Oval Office than an afterlife cruise ship. So when you read "heaven" in your Bible, you shouldn't think about an abode of souls first. You should think politically—*the place from which the king of the universe reigns and makes his decrees.*

This is why Paul said, "Our citizenship is in heaven."[8] He wasn't talking about life after death. He was talking about ultimate political allegiance. He, even as a Roman citizen, gave his ultimate allegiance to King Jesus, not Caesar.

Writing this to a Roman colony such as Philippi was nothing short of treason. If you've ever wondered why so many Christians were executed—despite practicing nonviolence, paying their taxes, caring for the sick, and giving to the needy—it was because Rome never received their chief allegiance. Christians understood that the Roman emperor's throne was too *small* for their king. Sure, they'd give Caesar their taxes. They'd serve him with excellence. They'd obey his laws faithfully. But they'd never give him their deepest loyalty, obedience, devotion, and hope. That was for King Jesus alone.

Caesar and his proxies could not bear this. They demanded that Christians give fidelity to Caesar over Christ. The Christians refused. And so, the Romans killed Christians in droves as traitors.

No Christian can hope to weather our culture's tribal politics without keeping first things first: Jesus is king.

Your primary citizenship is in heaven. Yes, you are called to be a productive citizen of your earthly country, working for its welfare with excellence and passion. But like Tim Farron, you must know whom you serve. You must never forget your true hope.

And doing so requires you to resist temptation.

Two Temptations to Naturalize

The devil loves to naturalize citizens of heaven on earth. He tricks you into relinquishing your heavenly citizenship, primarily tempting you in two ways:

1. He'll tempt you to mix Jesus with partisanship.

You conflate the lamb with the donkey or the elephant, believing that your party holds the key to God's kingdom. Aside from the fact that this breaks the first two commandments (do not worship any other gods or any images of God), this thinking is also overly simplistic. It is hopelessly naive to expect any human system to approximate the kingdom of God.

2. He'll tempt you to relegate Jesus to "spiritual things."

You buy the lie that Jesus doesn't care about politics or this world. And that his holy, set-apart people shouldn't get bogged down with these things either. But you must never forget that Jesus made this world, and he died to rescue it.[9] His resurrection is the firstfruit of this world's resurrection and renewal.[10] Jesus cares about this world.

Thankfully there is another way. Like the Israelites who left behind their golden calves, we can leave behind our elephants and donkeys.

I'm not saying that you cannot register as a Republican or Democrat, or even identify with one party over another. I'm saying that you must relativize your commitment to your party. It must always be second (or even better, fourth or fifth or sixth) to Jesus. You must never sacrifice your witness for the sake of a political win. You must never allow your party's platform or interest to shape your ethics and beliefs more than Jesus's teachings do. Where your party leaves behind Jesus's politic and ethics, you must leave behind your party.

You must never allow your party's platform or interest to shape your ethics and beliefs more than Jesus's teachings do.

One reason that Christians struggle to let go of their political idols is because they've failed to see the politic at the center of the gospel: Jesus is king.

The King Jesus Gospel

When Jesus preached the gospel, he repeated one phrase again and again: "the kingdom of God."

Although modern evangelicals tend to see this as reference to the afterlife, that's not precisely what Jesus meant. The kingdom of God refers to God's reign. And Jesus preached the good news that, through him, God's reign was finally returning to earth.[11]

If we were ancient people, the word choice would clue us into this fact because the term *gospel* comes from the vocabulary of ancient politics. In the first century, a gospel was typically the "good news" that a new king had ascended the throne and that an evil enemy had been defeated.

For example, an inscription from 9 BC describes the birthday of Augustus Caesar—the guy in charge when Jesus was born—as "the beginning of *the gospel*."[12] It goes on to claim that Caesar was "God manifest" and the "savior" of the world, who had come to "put an end to war." Caesar "fulfilled all the hopes of earlier times." That certainly *does* sound like good news!

So as you might imagine, it was an act of ridiculous political bravery for a Jewish rabbi to march around a Roman province announcing the gospel of a different kingdom! Yet Jesus did exactly that.

The prophet Isaiah foretold this announcement. He envisioned a day when a gospel would be preached to a broken world. What was that gospel according to Isaiah? It was the good news that "your God reigns."[13]

Jesus taught that the reign of God was coming through him: sins would be forgiven, bodies would be healed, and salvation would be offered freely by God's grace, not by human work. Jesus was the king, foretold by Isaiah, who would truly accomplish what Caesar's propogandists attributed to their emperor.

In John's gospel, it's clear that the Jews were able to get Jesus crucified precisely because he claimed to be a king. This was treason. Jewish leaders chided Pilate, "If you release this man, you are not Caesar's friend. Everyone who makes himself a king opposes Caesar." When Pilate asked the crowd, "Shall I crucify your King?" they didn't respond by saying, "He never claimed to be a king!" They responded, "We have no king but Caesar." And as was common practice, Roman soldiers posted Jesus's capital crime on his cross: "King of the Jews."[14]

Jesus was crucified for announcing the good news of the kingdom—which was God's, not Caesar's!

This is why the apostles presented Jesus as the descendant of King David in their first sermons.[15] They were calling their fellow Jews to give their allegiance to Jesus, the true son of God, not Caesar.

The call still applies to Christians today. You can make Trump, Biden, or Harris—or whoever—your hope for the salvation and transformation of the world. You can give the donkey or the elephant your allegiance. *Or* you can give King Jesus your loyalty. But you can't have it both ways.

So how do we give Jesus our allegiance?

A New Oath

We are saved freely, as a gift of God. No one can earn his favor. Instead, the apostle Paul said that we receive this gift through "faith."[16] Often, when we hear the word *faith*, we think of mere mental assent: believing in Jesus. But we know that this cannot be the full meaning of faith because even the demons believe.[17]

True faith is deeper than assent. It's assent *with loyalty*. Indeed, the Greek word for *faith* could also be translated as "allegiance."

In other words, following Jesus entails pledging our allegiance to him. This is an inherently political act, which is why foreigners must make a pledge of loyalty to become naturalized citizens of the United States. Here's part of that pledge:

> I hereby declare, on oath, that I absolutely and entirely renounce and abjure all allegiance and fidelity to any foreign prince, potentate, state, or sovereignty, of whom or which I have heretofore been a subject or citizen; that I will support and defend the Constitution and laws of the United States of America against all enemies, foreign and domestic; that I will bear true faith and allegiance to the same; that I will bear arms on behalf of the United States when required by the law ... so help me God.[18]

Have you pledged allegiance to Jesus?

Tim Farron gave up his career to remain true to his oath of allegiance to Jesus. Are you prepared to do the same?

Sometimes I wish our adult baptisms included a variation of the pledge of American citizenship:

I hereby declare, on oath, that I absolutely and entirely renounce all allegiance and fidelity to all other presidents, political parties, tribes, nations, states, powers, sins, idols, relationships, and even my own self. I pledge my true faith and allegiance to King Jesus. I pledge my life, my time, my wealth, my relationships, my desires, my work, my possessions, my strength, my power, my interests, my politics, my thoughts to the service of King Jesus above everything else. I am from this point forward a slave to none except King Jesus. I am an ambassador of his good news, sent out for his purposes in the world, called to share in his sacrificial kingship, empowered by his Spirit, in order to build his kingdom on earth as in heaven.

Make that pledge today. Start every day on your knees before King Jesus, promising him your allegiance at home, at work, and everywhere in between. Yes, we will all fall short of it, but thankfully, Jesus is a forgiving king who graciously empowers us to change slowly over time.

The political tribes of the left and the right desperately want the allegiance you owe to Jesus. If you give it to them, you will be sucked into their battles and lies. But if you give your heart's deepest allegiance to Jesus, you will be set free from political tribalism in order to pursue the neighbor-loving politic of the kingdom of God.

Discussion and Reflection Questions

1. In the past, how have you given allegiance to a political, cultural, or workplace tribe *over* Jesus?

2. How does the politic of Jesus's kingdom *challenge* your preferred party's platform, character, or posture?

3. What's a practical way you can remind yourself to give your allegiance to the lamb every day?

Chapter 13

You Admit When You Don't Know

She was kind, but concerned: "Why do you keep discussing issues of racial justice and unity in Bible study? I *agree* that these things matter, but you're a pastor. Your job is to preach the gospel. Not this social justice stuff. I've read the New Testament more times than I can count, and I've never read one word talking about race in the church! So why do you talk about it? Don't you think the Bible knows best?"

I smiled through gritted teeth. She was confident. And she was *fantastically* wrong. Jesus envisioned a multi-racial, multi-lingual kingdom.[1] This vision shocked his disciples. They never imagined that the kingdom would include Jews and Gentiles. So perhaps it's not a surprise that the first major problem the early church faced was disunity between *ethnic* groups.[2]

But back to my conversation with the woman in my Bible study. It wasn't the first time I faced undue confidence. All pastors experience this. After Keith preached a sermon challenging rapture theology, one congregant wrote this in an email: "Keith clearly doesn't know his Bible. He doesn't realize there are about a hundred scriptures that talk about this event." He was confident. And he was wrong. Even those who believe in the rapture would admit there are only *two* passages that discuss it.

Overconfidence isn't limited to emails. Someone I follow on Twitter posted this: "Jesus taught that love is love. That white supremacy is real. That gender is a construct. That religion is toxic. That sex is good. That without justice there is no peace."

In other words, Jesus time traveled to the twenty-first century, memorized the progressive platform, time traveled back, and then taught it like it was his idea. It was confidently retweeted by thousands of people, even though many of the things on that list cannot be found in the Bible or Jesus's teachings. Some are explicitly contradicted.

Confidence is attractive. We like confident people. We love confident leaders. The world tells you to be confident in yourself.

And few things make us more confident than agreeing with our tribe.

How Tribalism Fuels Overconfidence

Proverbs warns us, "Enthusiasm without knowledge is no good."[3] The Sons of Korah put the risk of overconfidence more starkly:

> This is the path of those who have foolish
>   confidence....
> Like sheep they are appointed for Sheol;
>   death shall be their shepherd,
> and the upright shall rule over them in the
>   morning.
> Their form shall be consumed in Sheol, with no
>   place to dwell.[4]

Ouch. What I find interesting about this passage is that it acknowledges the tribal dynamics behind foolish confidence. The Sons of Korah don't address a *lone* fool, but a *flock* of sheep misled by a foolish shepherd. It's a *tribe* of fools.

The psalmists see that tribalism often gives you false confidence in things you don't actually know. You assume that, because the tribe says it, it must be true. And you're literally hardwired to do this, by the way, because using your brain takes a massive amount of energy. Despite only making up 2 percent of your total body mass, your brain consumes about 20 percent of your body's energy every day. Our ancestors, up until the last hundred years, faced constant caloric deficits. The most efficient way to conserve energy was to think less. Or more accurately, to think *with*. Trusting your tribe's perspective saves calories and keeps you safely enmeshed in your tribal network.

This isn't all bad. There is no way a single human could know *everything*. That's why we store knowledge in community. Plumbers know how plumbing works. Coders know how apps work. Lenders know how loans work. We trust the community to get it right.

This is even true for things we think we know. For example, you likely *know* that plants create energy using photosynthesis. But unless you're a plant biologist, you probably can't explain how photosynthesis works. In other words, your *knowledge* of photosynthesis is actually *trust* in the scientific community.

Tribalism preys on this helpful feature of the human psyche. You're hardwired to trust what the tribe says about "fact" and "fiction," "right" and "wrong."

In other words, tribalism tends to make us all overconfident about what we know and what we think we know.

Which takes us back to the Sons of Korah and their stark warning: confidence in the wrong tribe can lead you down dark paths. To avoid that destiny, you must learn to admit when you don't know something. Unfortunately, this is incredibly challenging because the *less* you know, the *more* confident you are likely to feel.

Incompetence Breeds Confidence

Charles Darwin wrote, "Ignorance more frequently begets confidence than does knowledge." Anyone who's been sixteen experienced this firsthand: you were often wrong, but never in doubt.

Recent research has proved Darwin correct. The *lower* one's competence is, the *higher* their confidence is. It's called the Dunning-Kruger effect: when your confidence exceeds your competence.[5]

For example, a group of managers were asked to rate their managerial competence. At the same time, the managers were observed and rated by an outsider based on their *actual* performance. The managers who received the lowest marks for competence were also the *most* confident in their managerial skills. The most competent managers were the least confident in their managerial skills.

In the original Dunning-Kruger study, researchers asked people to rate their competence in a subject area. People who knew absolutely nothing about a subject area gave themselves the lowest ratings for competence. That makes sense. So perhaps you'd expect that subject area experts gave themselves the highest competence ratings. Surprisingly, experts never gave themselves the highest marks for competence. Instead, the experts tended to accurately self-assess their competence against other experts.

The group that gave themselves the highest ratings of competence were amateurs: people who know *something* about a subject but are not experts in it.

This means that amateurs are the most prone to *overconfidence.* Those who know the basics of American history are the most overconfident about their historical knowledge. Those who know the basics of the Bible are most overconfident about their biblical knowledge. Those who know the basics of immigration policy are most overconfident about their knowledge of immigration policy.

Amateurs are also the most prone to overconfident errors. Jesus was right: "Whoever exalts himself will be humbled, and whoever humbles himself will be exalted."[6]

Unfortunately, people committed to a political or cultural tribe tend to have amateur-level knowledge on a lot of subjects. The tribe introduces them to a topic and tells them what to think. An expert could lay out all the countervailing evidence and nuances, but an amateur does not know them. The amateur is oblivious. *That's the nub of the problem.* You don't know when the Dunning-Kruger effect is taking place precisely because you can't be an expert in everything.

So is there any way to avoid overconfidence?

I'm glad you asked.

Join the Dunning-Kruger Club

Jesus encouraged humility, not overconfidence. One way to grow in humility is to be humbled. In his book *Think Again*, Adam Grant offered a Dunning-Kruger self-assessment.[7] I took it, and I was humbled. I welcome you to join the humbled club by answering these questions (I even added a Bible one!):

- Why is English the official language of the United States?
- On which spaceflight did humans first see the Great Wall of China?
- How many people did Paul personally kill before he became a Christian?
- What job did Walt Disney have before he drew Mickey Mouse?
- Why were women burned at the stake in Salem?
- Why did Cuban immigrants increase joblessness in Miami?

Which answers do you feel the most confident about? On a scale of one to ten, how do you rate your overall competence in those subject areas?

Once you're finished, assess your result. But before you do, let me apologize. These are all trick questions. If you gave an answer to *any* of them, you are susceptible to the Dunning-Kruger effect because they are all based on false premises.

The United States has no official language. The Great Wall of China isn't visible from space. Paul did not personally kill anyone. Walt Disney didn't draw Mickey Mouse. Women were not burned at the stake in Salem. Mass Cuban immigration had no impact on native-born employment in Miami.

So now that you, like me, know that you're susceptible to overconfidence, here's the first lesson: don't believe everything you think. As Proverbs says, "The way of a fool is right in his own eyes."[8]

DON'T BELIEVE EVERYTHING YOU THINK.

Here's the second lesson: don't believe everything your tribe tells you to think. Paul wrote, "Do not be conformed to this world, but be transformed by the renewal of your mind."[9]

Instead, embrace the path of Christlike humility: admit what you don't know.

Knowing What You Don't Know

Let's get practical. To become humble about your knowledge, begin by dividing it into three areas.

1. Things I know I don't know
2. Things I think I know
3. Things I know I know

Category 1 will always be the largest. Category 3 will always be the smallest. Category 2 will always be the most dangerous. Why? Because category 2 is precisely where we easily fall into the trap of confident incompetence.

Thankfully, the first step toward humility is simple: honesty.

The next time you're in a conversation, admit when you don't have enough information. If you're speaking to someone with more expertise, try listening. See what you can learn. You might even discover that you're *wrong*, which isn't bad because you'll leave the conversation closer to the truth. If you're speaking to someone who knows as much as you, or less than you, don't press beyond your knowledge. In a debate, it's always best to choose humility over victory.

For example, during the pandemic I heard a *lot* of nonexperts debating the effectiveness of masks, quarantines, and vaccines. When they asked my opinion, I always told them, "I'm not sure what to think on this, but here's what I am sure about: my last biology class was in tenth grade, so I have no business joining a conversation about immunology. I will trust the expert consensus, knowing full well that it might change in retrospect."

Sometimes people would admit that they were in the same boat. Others would demur and prove that they knew more than the experts by showing me their YouTube history, full of videos by their hand-picked COVID gurus. The few people I knew with *actual* expertise in medicine and public health shed light on my own perspective, though (as experts tend to do) they were careful about overstating their knowledge. But most people just ignored me, parading their pandemic tribe's position as though it were gospel truth.

There's no shame in admitting that you don't know. It's humble. And that's Christlike.

When Keith interviewed Philip Yancey on our podcast, he asked him if there was anything he would change about the twenty-five books he's written. What Philip said was remarkable.

"I might add this little phrase, a lot more often: *'but I could be wrong.'* Because when you get older you realize, *I could be wrong*. It's helpful to add that so the reader can make up his own mind."[10]

Yancey was right. You not only need to admit when your knowledge is *insufficient*; you also need to admit that you're often wrong. I know I am. And of course, you should always go one step further: when you discover you're wrong, admit it.

This, too, is supremely Christlike.

Jesus Changed His Mind

Mark's gospel tells the story of Jesus and his disciples leaving the primarily Jewish province of Judea to take a trip northwest to the province of Syria. He was probably looking for a break from the crowds and knew few people would recognize him there. But when a Syrophoenician woman saw Jesus and his disciples eating, she fell down at Jesus's feet and begged him to free her daughter from demonic possession.

> And [Jesus] said to her, "Let the children be fed first, for it is not right to take the children's bread and throw it to the dogs." But she answered him, "Yes, Lord; yet even the dogs under the table eat the children's crumbs." And he said to her, "For this statement you may go your way; the demon has left your daughter." And she went home and found the child lying in bed and the demon gone.[11]

How do we make sense of this jarring scene (that some people would like scrubbed from the Gospels)? Jesus corrected the woman, then she corrected him, and then Jesus *changed his mind.*

Some scholars say that he was teaching his disciples a lesson: he spoke what *they* were thinking to show *them* that *they* needed to rethink their assumption that the gospel was for Jews alone.

But I tend to take this story at face value. Jesus was fully God *and* fully human. Luke said that Jesus *grew* in wisdom.[12] So is it crazy to think that he revised his position on issues from time to time? Isn't that part of wisdom?[13]

Whichever view you hold, Jesus shows that there is no shame in changing your mind and admitting that you were previously wrong. He listened to the challenge of someone who disagreed with him. He changed his perspective. In doing so, he rejected the common but false assumptions of his own ethnic tribe and asserted a new standard (which actually fit the Old Testament quite well): the bread of life is for all people, *even Gentiles.*

Intellectual humility does not lead to defeat; it leads to the truth. Proverbs gets it right: "Humility comes before honor."[14]

The only way to pick truth over tribe is to humbly admit that your tribe doesn't have the corner on truth and neither do you. In fact, discovering truth is a humble and humbling process.

We all like looking omni-intelligent, omni-knowing, and omni-correct. But God, the only truly omniscient one, did not design us that way. God designed you to have limits. He designed you to *not* know. He designed you to discover. To learn. To rethink. To explore. When God gave Adam and Eve the mission to expand Eden, he implicitly gave them a calling to make new discoveries, build new things, and learn new ideas.

GOD DESIGNED YOU TO HAVE LIMITS. HE DESIGNED YOU TO _NOT_ KNOW. HE DESIGNED YOU TO DISCOVER. TO LEARN. TO RETHINK. TO EXPLORE.

God made you to be you, not God. So embrace your limits. You've got an eternity of learning (and rethinking) ahead of you.

Discussion and Reflection Questions

1. When you admit that you don't know something, or that you got something wrong, what emotions do you feel?

2. Name one thing that falls into each of these categories: (a) things you know you *don't* know; (b) things you *think* you know; (c) things you *know* you know.

3. How have you shown overconfidence about things that fall into the "things you *think* you know" category?

4. God doesn't expect you to know everything. He didn't design you to know everything. How would your life change if you embraced this truth more thoroughly?

Chapter 14

YOU CROSS TRIBAL LINES

There is nothing new about the "us vs. them" narrative that fuels tribalistic antagonism. It has been with us since time began. A brief jaunt through American history shows that vicious attacks are common.

- In 1856, Senator Charles Sumner was nearly beaten to death with a cane on the floor of the United States Senate by another senator who was upset with his speech against slavery.[1]
- A political opponent publicly mocked Abraham Lincoln as a "hatchet-faced nutmeg dealer."[2] (In case you were wondering: a "nutmeg dealer" was a term meaning a "con man.")
- Billboards in Alabama showed Martin Luther King in a class, falsely claiming it was a "communist training school."[3]

"Us vs. them" has been around since Adam blamed Eve and Cain killed Abel. Jesus came to reconcile people not only to God but also to one another. His teachings dismantled the belief structures that created and fomented tribal division. Yet, even after following Jesus for over a year, his disciples still thought in "us vs. them" categories, and they asked Jesus to punish their enemies.

When Samaritan villagers didn't give Jesus the welcome his disciples thought he deserved, they were outraged. James and John asked, "Lord, do you want us to call fire down from heaven to destroy them?"[4]

You can't help but wonder, *What happened to turning the other cheek and loving your enemy?*

But you can probably identify with their suspicion and judgmentalism. We all find it easy to turn against "them," if for no other reason than they are not "us."

Jesus and the disciples were passing through the Samaritan village on the way to Jerusalem, where his followers *expected* Jesus to overthrow the Romans and establish his military kingdom on earth. Since God defeated Israel's enemies in the past, wasn't it logical to believe he would do it again in the present? The disciples struggled to understand that Jesus was doing something different.

Instead, Jesus came to offer scandalous grace to *everyone*. Yes, even to the Samaritans. Yes, even to the "them" in your life.

Do You Know Your Enemy?

How many Samaritans did James and John know?

It's safe to say not many. Maybe none. The Samaritans were half-Jew and half-Gentile. They lived in their own villages. They once worshipped in their own temple (which Jews destroyed over a

century before Jesus's ministry). And they had their own scriptures
(Samaritans only used the first five books of the Hebrew Bible).

For Jews, Samaritans were the worst kind of "them" because,
unlike the pagan Gentiles who were ignorant of Jewish laws,
Samaritans should have known better. They corrupted what was
true and good about Judaism.

That explains why, on another occasion, the disciples were
appalled that Jesus initiated a conversation with a Samaritan
woman. Or why Jesus's story about a *good* Samaritan shocked his
listeners.

Jews didn't mix with Samaritans. So as a result, Jews didn't really
know Samaritans. They lived in a cultural and ideological bubble.

It's easy to demonize people you don't know. I grew up in a
political household. My mom and dad were leaders in state politics.
Before retiring from public life, Mom was a fierce liberal and Dad a
conservative Democrat. But because of their professions, they knew
people across the political spectrum. It was natural for those people
to end up at our house for a party of some sort. (Sometimes I was
recruited to be the bartender, and the next morning I reported on
how much each guest had to drink!)

Being close to the action meant that I saw firsthand that the
righteous and the unrighteous can be found in both political parties.
The line between good and evil didn't cut *between* parties. It cut
through both parties.

THE LINE BETWEEN GOOD AND EVIL DIDN'T CUT
BETWEEN PARTIES. IT CUT THROUGH BOTH PARTIES.

My parents knew this, so they modeled friendship, civility, and kindness toward people whose political ideology was far from their own. They never excluded someone from our house because of how he or she voted on a particular issue. There was never a "them" because they knew good people on both sides.

Do you know your enemy? Do you know that you can find good people in your "them"? Or do you live in a bubble, where you most interact with people who think like you?

You Probably Live in a Bubble

In our divided world, it is getting easier to live like the Jews and Samaritans—in a cultural, ideological, and political bubble. Pauline Kael, a film critic for the *New Yorker*, said she only knew one person who voted for Richard Nixon in the 1972 election, despite Nixon winning 60.7 percent of the popular vote.[5] His opponent, George McGovern, won only one state, and that wasn't even the state Kael lived in![6]

Election results reveal that, today, even more Americans live in ideological bubbles.

In 2020, there were 1,726 landslide counties.[7] A landslide county is one in which a presidential candidate beat their opponent by at least 20 percent. In other words, it's a county where most people share the same political allegiance. That means that 57 percent of all counties in the United States are decisively red or blue. So odds are that you live in a county where most people share your politics.

That might not sound crazy until you realize that just 40 years ago, in 1980, there were 391 landslide counties. Only 12 percent of

American counties were decisively red or blue. In 1980, odds were
that you lived in a county with a diversity of political allegiances.

How did this happen?

As far back as 2008, author Bill Bishop has been pointing
out that we've been choosing to live around people like us. In his
book, *The Big Sort*, he said it's not because people move in search
of like-minded voters. Instead, interests, values, and lifestyles map
predictably onto voting patterns.[8]

In fact, your political allegiances even shape where you shop.
You can accurately predict how people will vote based on which
retail outlets they live near. Republicans live near Tractor Supply,
Cracker Barrel, Hobby Lobby, and Bass Pro, while Democrats
live near Whole Foods, Lululemon, Urban Outfitters, and Apple
stores.[9]

While it is fun to conjecture why each party loves certain retail
ers, it all points to a bigger problem: How can we trust people we
don't know? The answer is obvious: we don't. We create false allegations and conspiracy theories about the other side to explain things
we can't understand. If you don't personally know people who voted
for the winning candidate, then maybe that's a sign that something
nefarious happened to influence the election?

Perhaps it is no surprise that both sides make faulty assumptions
about the other side. According to recent studies:

- Democrats estimate that 44 percent of
  Republicans make at least $250,000 a year, but
  only 2 percent make that much money.

- Democrats believe that only 40 percent of Republicans agree with the statement "Many Muslims are good Americans," but 66 percent do.
- Democrats think that only 50 percent of Republicans recognize that "racism still exists in America," but 80 percent do.
- Democrats estimate that only 50 percent of Republicans believe "properly controlled immigration can strengthen America," but in reality, 90 percent of Republicans do.
- Republicans estimate only 50 percent of Democrats are proud to be American, but in reality, 80 percent are.
- Republicans estimate 66 percent of Democrats favor open borders, but only 30 percent do.
- Republicans estimate that 46 percent of Democrats are black, but only 25 percent are.
- Republicans think 38 percent of Democrats identify as LGBTQ, but only 6 percent do.[10]

Republicans and Democrats think of their political opponents as being more extreme than they really are. Sadly, the more you dig into the research, the more you uncover a depressing picture. The same studies found that the *better* educated someone is on political issues, the more likely he or she is to be *wrong* about the other side. People who don't follow the news have a more accurate understanding of their opponents' views. Maybe this tells us that we don't just need more information about the issues.

Jesus knows what we really need: relationships with people who disagree with us.

The Curated Life

The disciples didn't know any Samaritans, but they knew a lot *about* them. They didn't have any Samaritan friends. They didn't shop at the same (kosher) markets or attend the same weddings, bar mitzvahs, or Passover celebrations. So where did they get their information about the Samaritans?

The more we live in a bubble with people like us, the more we depend on the words of others to tell us what "they" are like.

In Jesus's day, this happened through gossip. In our day, it comes through media.

The *Daily Me* is a digital news curator that allows its customers to pick the news according to their personal beliefs. If the *New York Times*'s motto is "All the News That's Fit to Print," then the *Daily Me*'s approach is "All the News That Fits Your Perspective."

And why not? Cord cutting is on the rise as people demand more control over what they watch. Thanks to iTunes, I don't have to buy whole albums. I can buy the individual songs I choose. So why shouldn't I be able to customize my newsfeed to fit my beliefs?

Our news and neighborhoods aren't the only things we curate to fit our perspectives. Facebook's algorithms are designed to give you more of what you like—stories about how the other side is composed of either Hitlers, Marxists, or Fundamentalists who ruin families, society, schools, churches, democracy, and/or the soul of America.

As we discussed previously, Facebook executives know the company contributes to polarization. "Our algorithms exploit the human brain's attraction to divisiveness," read a slide from a 2018 presentation. "If left unchecked," it warned, Facebook would feed users "more and more divisive content in an effort to gain user attention and increase time on the platform."[11]

Various tweaks designed by Facebook engineers to de-escalate arguments or expose people to more diverse groups were eventually rejected out of fear that the interventions were "paternalistic."

But those offering the warning within Facebook were right. When you interact with people who share your same political and cultural perspective, you become more extreme and hardened in your positions.

Harvard professor Cass Sunstein pointed to research that examined how ideological echo chambers affect our beliefs.[12] The conclusions are not all that surprising. The more you talk to people who agree with you, the more confident and strident you become. People won't moderate their views or seek common ground if they primarily interact with those who are already a part of their political and cultural tribe.

The more time you spend in the echo chamber, the more you see "them" as the enemy.

When a Trumpite Plows Your Driveway

Virginia Heffernan's Trump-supporting neighbor had the audacity to plow her driveway without being asked. Instead of being appreciative, the political columnist for the *Los Angeles Times* was suspicious of the "act of aggressive niceness."[13] Using her public forum, she insinuated that her neighbor was a racist and a Nazi while comparing him to Hezbollah, a terrorist organization that takes care of people in its own tribe while murdering the infidels.

Heffernan decided she would acknowledge the plowing with "a wave and a thanks," but she wasn't "ready to knock on the door with a covered dish yet." How big of her. She said she does hold out hope that her neighbors—and by extension the over 74 million Americans who voted for President Trump in 2020—can get back in her good graces. Groveling, repenting, and voting for a Democrat would be more appreciated than shoveling.

Virginia Heffernan incriminated herself while casting aspersions on her neighbor's motives: clearly he only shoveled her driveway because she's white. "Loving your neighbor," she wrote, "is evidently much easier when your neighborhood is full of people just like you."[14]

She then accused the Trumpite of living in a bubble with people who look like him. But hasn't she proved the opposite? If anyone needs to escape the echo chamber, it's her. She is able to demonize her neighbor precisely because she doesn't have relationships with people who voted for Trump.

Jesus Bursts the Bubble

Jesus won't let you stay in your bubble. He will bring you face to face with "them"—the people you think of as your political, ideological, or cultural enemies, who nonetheless are *also* his followers. And Jesus has the audacity to tell you that you have more in common with the "them" who follow him than you do with those in your tribe who *don't* follow him.

Consider just two of Jesus's twelve disciples: Simon the Zealot and Matthew the tax collector.

Simon's nickname, "The Zealot," signaled that he was part of a Jewish nationalist group that championed violent rebellion against Rome. Matthew's designation as "the tax collector" tells us that he was a Roman sympathizer. Tax collectors collaborated with Rome and sold out their own kinsmen for personal gain. These two men were further apart politically than Ted Cruz and Alexandria Ocasio-Cortez. They weren't the kind of different that complemented each other. They were the kind that tried to kill each other.

But when they responded to Jesus's call and began following him, they joined a community that relativized their political, ideological, and cultural differences. It's not that following Jesus led them to agree on every issue—there aren't necessarily "Christian positions" on all the hot topics of their day or ours. But loyalty to Jesus superseded their loyalty to every other movement.

In the end, Jesus changed them both. Matthew ceased to be a Roman sympathizer. Simon set down his sword.

You should feel more at home with people who share your faith than people who share your politics. Christians are a band of natural enemies brought together by the love of Jesus.

You should feel more at home with people who share your faith than people who share your politics.

Living in ideological bubbles allows us to believe the worst about those who belong to a different tribe. But when we build relationships with those same people inside the church, we see that, like us, they are more complex than the media portray them. The Trump supporter living next door volunteers at a homeless shelter. The socialist down the street brings you a meal when you're sick. Both love their families. Both care about their communities.

The End of "Them"

James and John got a lot of things wrong.

They were wrong about the Samaritans. Their request for fiery judgment on the Samaritans only earned a rebuke from Jesus. To their surprise, Samaritans responded in faith to him and were among his first followers after his resurrection. Eventually James and John became friends with the Samaritan "them" whom they once wanted to destroy.

James and John were also wrong about Jesus's ultimate goal. Jesus wasn't going to Jerusalem to defeat his enemies, but to die for *them*. That's good news, because it turns out that the only divide between "us" and "them" that matters is the divide between a holy God and sinful humans. If those are the only two options, we know where we belong without Jesus.

James and John were wrong about discipleship. Jesus's followers don't call down judgment on "them." We lay down our lives for "them," just as Jesus laid down his life for us when we were his enemy.

I've been wrong about a lot of people. I'm sure I'll be wrong again. That's why I constantly try to remind myself: *Jesus loves the "them" in my life. And I should too.*

Who are the "them" Jesus is calling you to love the way he does?

Discussion and Reflection Questions

1. What are the negative assumptions you make about people who disagree with you?

2. What makes it challenging for you to step across tribal lines? What do you fear losing? Who do you fear offending? What do you fear owning?

3. Jesus stepped across tribal lines to reach you. Who is he calling you to step across tribal lines to reach? How could you do this, practically?

Chapter 15

You Listen

I thought I was a good leader. *Until I started doing exit interviews.*

"I really enjoyed being on the team," she told me diplomatically, "but I was never sure if I was doing the right thing. I know you wanted to give me freedom to my job as I saw fit, but it never felt like a world of possibilities. It felt like an endless fog I couldn't find my way out of. I was never sure whether I was doing a good job or even the right thing."

Ouch.

I smiled and *mhmmed* my way through it, but I didn't believe her. That night, I told my wife that she was trying to cover up her insecurities about her job performance. She wanted to be micromanaged so she wouldn't have to take responsibility for her schedule. She wasn't cut out for a team of self-starters.

My wife smiled and *mhmmed her way through it*, but she saw through my defensiveness. I was the insecure one. She told me I was wrong. Clarity *is* important. People need feedback. An employee seeking to use her time on the right things is a *good* employee.

Over the next year, I conducted two more exit interviews. Both of them repeated—almost verbatim—the same ideas as the first person. I considered whether they were in a conspiracy together. And then I allowed my fragile ego to shatter. I accepted the truth: *I'm not a good manager. If I don't listen to them, I will only get worse.*

By God's grace, I listened, began to read books on management, and eventually sought out a coach who taught me basic management principles—most of which I'd been neglecting. It was humbling. But it was also necessary growth.

The cost of *not* listening is stagnation, pride, and a lack of self-awareness.

This reminds me of a strange story from the Roman philosopher Seneca. He wrote about a woman who was blind but refused to admit it. No matter where people took her, she claimed that she was simply in a very dark room. She would not listen to anyone who told her otherwise.[1]

Fast-forward eighteen centuries, and a psychiatrist named Gabriel Anton met a woman with a very similar condition. Vision tests showed that his patient, Ursula, had seriously impaired eyesight. Eventually, she became fully blind. But when he met with her, she claimed that she could see everything. He would describe objects in the office, and she calmly explained that she could see all of them. If he claimed an object was in the room, which was not, Ursula claimed that she could see it.

When Anton explained that he had made up the object, and that she was in fact blind, Ursula would vehemently deny it. She wouldn't listen. He eventually discovered that she was *truly* blind to her blindness. The condition, now called Anton syndrome, is caused by damage to the cerebral cortex and basal ganglia.[2]

Something similar happens to you when you refuse to listen.

People see your blind spots. They try to alert you. But because you're blind to your blind spots, you write off their concern. And in doing so, you condemn yourself to a stunted, arrogant, unreflective life.

This is probably why the Bible's wisdom literature is *fixated* on the importance of listening. Proverbs challenges its audience to listen more than thirty times.

It describes the benefits of listening: "Whoever ignores instruction despises himself, but he who listens to reproof gains intelligence."[3] And it warns about the costs of ignoring: "I did not listen to the voice of my teachers or incline my ear to my instructors. I am at the brink of utter ruin in the assembled congregation."[4] A truly wise person can see the tremendous *value* of correction: "Like a gold ring or an ornament of gold is a wise reprover to a listening ear."[5] While "a fool is right in his own eyes."[6]

There are few things more valuable than the opinion of someone *who disagrees with you.* One of the greatest gifts God can give you is a friend who sees the world differently than you. Such a friend will see your blind spots and help you grow.

ONE OF THE GREATEST GIFTS GOD CAN GIVE YOU IS A FRIEND WHO SEES THE WORLD DIFFERENTLY THAN YOU.

Unfortunately, tribalism makes it almost impossible for you to hear them.

How Groups Make Us Deaf

Solomon was known for his wisdom, but his son Rehoboam was not. After his father's death, the people of Israel came to Rehoboam and asked him to lighten their labor and taxation. Solomon's former advisers told Rehoboam to listen to the people.

But Rehoboam wasn't interested in listening to their opinion.

Rehoboam wanted the opinion of *his* tribe: his friends. They understood that less taxation meant less wealth for Rehoboam and his court, so they encouraged a different approach: *increase the burden or the people will think you're weak.* Rehoboam's friends even wrote a speech for him to deliver. It's a crude joke followed by violent threats: "My little finger is thicker than my father's thighs. And now, whereas my father laid on you a heavy yoke, I will add to your yoke. My father disciplined you with whips, but I will discipline you with scorpions."[7]

Rather than quelling a revolt, Rehoboam fomented one with his brashness. In the end, Rehoboam lost ten of the twelve tribes of Israel. They formed a new confederation to the north under a new king, Jeroboam.

Groups make it easy to ignore wisdom.

The reason is simple to understand: if I believe that I alone am correct on a topic while everyone else is wrong, then I am probably a pathological narcissist (case in point: Pharaoh during the exodus). Normal people, however, find it easy to listen and change their minds when they're alone on an issue.

But what happens when a group of smart, nice people agree with you? Listening to outsiders suddenly becomes harder. After all, how could *we* be wrong?

Take modern academia: while college faculties are growing increasingly diverse in terms of gender and race (which is a good thing!), they're *also* becoming increasingly uniform in ideology. Like

Gabriel Anton's patient, they seem increasingly uninterested in listening to those who disagree with them.

New York Times columnist Nicholas Kristof put it well: "We're fine with people who don't look like us, as long they think like us."[8]

In response to Kristof's concerns, many professors responded with their own columns claiming matter-of-factly that universities are more progressive simply because progressivism is *true* and conservativism is *false*, and professors are too intelligent to believe falsehoods. One said, "The truth has a liberal slant." Another said, "How about we make faculties more diverse by hiring idiots?" Still another said, "Much of the 'conservative' worldview consists in ideas that are known empirically to be false."[9]

Baylor professor of sociology George Yancey found that at least 29 percent of university faculty members would actively resist hiring a member of the National Rifle Association.[10] Which of course begs the question: Does gun ownership categorically make someone "empirically false" or an "idiot"?

Of course not.

What if the truth is that universities are echo chambers and that a lack of ideological diversity decreases the rigor and the quality of their academic work? What if the truth is that no tribe likes to hear countervailing arguments that undermine their ability to blindly declare superiority?

Tribalism makes us all a bit like Rehoboam, glibly racing with our pack toward destruction. Leaving tribalism requires us to take the wisdom of Proverbs seriously: we *must* listen to those who contradict our tribe. To do that, you need to surround yourself with people who think differently. You need cognitive diversity.

The Benefits of Cognitive Diversity

The most effective organizations are diverse.[11] But what kind of diversity matters most for success?

You might expect that it's diversity of gender and ethnicity. But Alison Reynolds and David Lewis published research in the *Harvard Business Review* that found "no correlation between this type of diversity and performance."[12] But this doesn't mean that diversity *doesn't* matter. Reynolds and Lewis discovered that one form of diversity can make or break an organization: *cognitive diversity*. People with varied personalities, opinions, and perspectives. According to Reynolds and Lewis, if your organization *listens* to a diversity of opinions, your organization will flourish.

Here's why:

> **1. You'll Produce Better Ideas:** When you walk into a room of people who think the same way, decisions are easy. After all, there will only be a small number of similar options on the table. But when you walk into a room full of people who think differently, you must enter prepared, because opinions and options will vary wildly. You'll think more rigorously about every idea you produce, because you know you'll have to defend it. Even more importantly, you can expect to be presented with ideas you never could have imagined—which often outperform your own! Listening to diverse voices will increase your odds of producing high-quality ideas.

2. You'll Identify Problems Earlier: Every plan sounds great until you share it with someone else. A diverse group is more likely to see the holes in your thinking. While that's sometimes painful, wouldn't you prefer to be wrong *before* you get going rather than failing halfway in? Listening to diverse voices will help you avoid future mistakes.

3. You'll Serve More People: Most organizations try to serve a wide variety of people. The more your team represents the diverse people you serve—not just a small slice of it—the more likely you are to give them something they *actually* want. Listening to diverse voices maximizes your potential reach.

4. You'll Make Better Decisions: A diverse team brings a diverse set of values and decision-making styles to the table. Is it better to move quickly or slowly on this project? Does quantity or quality serve our goals better? Does fixing this problem require a new system or a quick fix? Our personalities often shape our responses to these questions—regardless of the issue at hand—which means we'll make a better decision if we have *more* personalities in the room voicing various perspectives.

I've learned most of this from personal experience. My team has a *lot* of cognitive diversity. One of our staff members loves Trump.

Another loves Obama. Our oldest team member is in his fifties. Our youngest is in her early twenties. Some of us are decisive. Others are methodical. Some of us grew up Christian. Others met Jesus later in life. Some care most about effectiveness. Others care most about aesthetics. Some of us like to move as fast as possible. Others want time to process.

I love this diversity because it gives our team *constant* opportunities to listen, rethink, and improve. If I only listened to *my* tribe, I know I would be a lot like Rehoboam: I'd brashly race into foolish decisions without fear of future costs. I'd be a partisan, palpably aware of my opponent's blind spots and blind to my own. I'd be— to use the language of Proverbs—a fool blindly skipping toward destruction.

Some of the best advice I've ever received came from people who disagreed with me on significant things. So I'm always asking myself, "Who do I need to listen to today?"—knowing that person is probably the last person I'd expect.

Who Do You Need to Listen To?

As a pastor, I run the risk of living in a Christian bubble. Most of the people I interact with on a daily basis are Christians. So I know that I need to actively seek out non-Christians so that I can listen to and learn from them.

What about you? Do you know which echo chambers you're living in? It's not enough to have a Republican friend or a Democrat friend. You need a friend you actually *hear*. In fact, there's an easy test to determine if you're *actually* listening to diverse voices: *When was the last time you changed your mind on an important issue?*

You should pride yourself on changing your mind because it's the only sure sign of listening. Proverbs is right: "The ear that listens to life-giving reproof will dwell among the wise. Whoever ignores instruction despises himself, but he who listens to reproof gains intelligence."[13]

If Jesus is calling you out of tribalism and into truth, diversity, and humility, then listening is a requisite skill to master.

Followers of Jesus know that they've been desperately wrong in the past. Paul wrote, "Formerly, when you did not know God, you were slaves to those who by nature are not gods."[14] In other words, every Christian on earth—at some point in their lives—got God wrong. And nothing should be easier to get *right* than the nature of God! As Paul wrote elsewhere, "What can be known about God is plain ... because God has shown it to them. For his invisible attributes, namely, his eternal power and divine nature, have been clearly perceived, ever since the creation of the world, in the things that have been made."[15]

No Christian came to know the truth about God by their own intellectual prowess. Jesus rescued you from your stupidity *by grace*. This reality should keep you humble. If you can get God wrong, you can get vaccines wrong. You can get racial justice wrong. You can get educational policy wrong.

But this reality should also give you freedom to listen and change without fear. From the start, Jesus's love for you was not contingent on your correctness—it was in spite of your incorrectness. He is not a heavenly SAT proctor, withholding his love from those who answer questions imperfectly. He is a gracious teacher, forgiving your errors and guiding you into the truth.

And one way Jesus loves to guide you into truth is through the voices of others. Don't let tribalism steal the joy of being wrong—that's the first step toward learning! Instead, let Jesus set you free from tribalism by embracing the beauty of listening.

Don't let tribalism steal the joy of being wrong.

Discussion and Reflection Questions

1. Recall a time when someone who thought differently than you disagreed with you. How did you respond?

2. How does listening to diverse voices make us wiser and more successful?

3. How has listening led you to a deeper understanding of the truth?

4. Who are the diverse voices Jesus is putting in your life to guide you to truth?

Chapter 16

You Join an Inclusive Tribe

The number three had a significant place in Peter's life. He denied Jesus three times. After his resurrection, Jesus asked Peter three times if he loved him. Three times Peter responded yes. And three times Jesus commissioned Peter to feed his sheep.

But Peter still had a lot to learn about which sheep belonged to Jesus.

Before Jesus ascended to heaven, he commissioned his followers to be his witnesses, starting in Jerusalem and, eventually, going to the ends of the earth. Peter started in Jerusalem. The problem, however, was that he *stayed* in Jerusalem.

You can imagine why he might have done so. Jerusalem was full of the people Peter felt most comfortable with—the people most like him ethnically and religiously. It took a wave of persecution to force him out. But even after that, wherever he traveled, he stuck around Jews.

So God decided to teach Peter that his love and grace extend to *everyone*. But this lesson was so far outside of Peter's expectations that God had to state it not once, not twice, but—you guessed it— three times.

An Unlikely Convert

Cornelius was a Gentile Roman military officer stationed in Caesarea. He received a vision from an angel, in which God told him to send for Peter, who was about forty miles south in Joppa. Cornelius was profoundly interested in God but had never heard of Jesus.

Unfortunately, the biggest obstacle for Cornelius's faith wasn't his doubts or personal sins. It was people like Peter—those who believed that Jesus was only interested in people "like me." Peter didn't have a category for someone like Cornelius—a *Gentile*—coming to faith and joining the people of God.

Thankfully, Cornelius obeyed the angel and sent some of his men to Joppa to bring Peter to him. But before Cornelius's men reached Peter, God needed to reach Peter.

God sent Peter a vision showing that he had abolished the food laws that kept Israel distinct from the Gentiles. Peter didn't have a category for that. The historical, cultural, and religious separation between Jews and Gentiles ran so deep that Peter couldn't imagine why a Jewish Messiah would want a relationship with a Gentile—much less how he could reconcile the two groups. Peter's incredulity explains why God gave him that same vision *three* times.

When Cornelius's men arrived, Peter left with them. Cornelius welcomed Peter warmly, but Peter was obviously uncomfortable. He awkwardly explained that Jewish law forbade Jews to associate with Gentiles. He only came because God had showed him a vision revealing that not only was all food clean but so were all people. In effect, Peter said, "God is up to something new, and I'm trying to figure it out."

But God wasn't up to anything new. Peter had fallen into a tribalistic mindset that kept him from seeing what had always been true:

Jesus came to call a diverse, multi-ethnic, multi-lingual, multinational group to follow him.

Jewish law might forbid befriending Gentiles, but God's law never did. Peter narrowed God's plan until it encompassed his tribe alone. Of course, we do the same thing when we think that God is for *my* tribe, *my* country, *my* people, and *my* party.

> ### JESUS CAME TO CALL A DIVERSE, MULTI-ETHNIC, MULTI-LINGUAL, MULTI-NATIONAL GROUP TO FOLLOW HIM.

But in Cornelius's house, Peter saw the true expansiveness of God's plan. Jesus was calling him (and Cornelius!) to join a bigger tribe—God's tribe—in which *everyone* was welcome.

Of course, most of us like this idea in theory, but it's hard in practice.

Unnecessary Division

Dr. C. W. Dawson is a great guy who always has a good story to tell. He pastors a mostly black church in Columbia, Missouri, where we both live. We first met during a season of heightened racial tension in our community. Columbia is less than two hours from Ferguson, Missouri, where Michael Brown was killed by Officer Darren Wilson on August 9, 2014. That police shooting, which came on the heels of a jury declaring George Zimmerman not guilty in the death of

Trayvon Martin, catalyzed protests for racial justice and raised the national profile of organizations like Black Lives Matter.

Our city is home to the University of Missouri, which, like most universities, has its own history of racial discrimination. In 2015, an activist group called Concerned Student 1950 called on the school and its president, Tim Wolfe, to confront past and present racism on campus.[1] The administration fumbled the issue, and soon, the campus was awash in protests and hunger strikes. The story went national when the Missouri football team threatened to boycott their game against Brigham Young University unless the university president resigned over his mishandling of the situation.

During this time, our church, The Crossing, worked hard to bring white and black pastors together to model a path forward for our community. We held monthly pastors' breakfasts, where we listened and learned from one another. I met Dr. Dawson at one of those breakfasts.

On occasion, we grabbed lunch together, which gave me a chance to hear more of his story. I always walked away from those conversations feeling as if I had learned something important. And I'm indebted to him for encouraging me to read James Cone and other authors who helped me better understand the black experience.

After the sermon on gender that led a local film festival to end our decade-long partnership (we told *that* story in chapter 4), Dr. Dawson reached out and said that he'd encouraged the local newspaper to invite me to write a column that would appear alongside his regular column. I was grateful because it gave our church an opportunity to share where we were coming from, but this time in a public forum, not a worship service.

C. W.'s column began with kind, supportive words for both me
and The Crossing.[2] He affirmed that we were good people doing
good things in the community even if (on this issue) we'd have to
"agree to disagree." I'll always remember him vouching for our character at a time when others were piling on and misrepresenting us to
stir up trouble.

After that, he explained why he disagreed with us. Dr. Dawson
attributed our different approaches to the topic of gender to our
cultural and historical paradigms: "Keith Simon is a Christocentric,
evangelical Christian committed to a white, western European,
Anglo-American understanding of God, the Bible, salvation,
authentic living, etc. Such is the paradigm out of which he operates,
and I respect that."[3]

He was explaining to his readers what theological tribe I'm a
part of and how that shaped my conclusions. He continued, "I, however, am an African American, theocentric Christian committed to
an African American understanding of God as Mother and Father,
a black hermeneutical method of interpreting the Bible that affirms
and includes the whole human race as the children of God and not
just Christians."[4]

In other words, he's part of a different theological tribe and,
therefore, arrived at different conclusions. Others—but not Dr.
Dawson—go further, claiming that these tribes are fundamentally
opposed. One is Christian. One is not.

In a conversation over sushi the following week, I told C. W.
that I don't consider black and white Christians to be part of different tribes. Biblically and theologically, I am in the same tribe as
Augustine, Athanasius, and Tertullian—who were all *African* church

fathers. I am in the same tribe as all the Jesus followers in the global south and every other part of the world. Following Jesus should not lead us to form parochial tribes around race or theology—instead, it should lead us to form a worldwide tribe that welcomes everyone and charitably dialogues over our differences.

Of course, this is an ideal that Christians rarely live up to, but Dr. Dawson and I ultimately agreed: We are brothers in the same tribe. We have sincere differences, and Jesus will hold us accountable for what we believe and what we teach. But we are not partisans of competing tribes. Dr. Dawson showed that unity by treating me charitably in public. I hope to always do the same for him.

Unknowing Disciple

Peter thought God endorsed his tribal approach to Gentiles. He didn't understand that God's original plan for his people included racial and ethnic diversity. In Genesis 12, God promised Abram that, through him, God would bless *all* the nations of the world. God rescued Israel from Pharaoh's Egypt so that the *whole world* would know his name.[5] And when Pharaoh relented, a diverse, "mixed multitude" left Egypt, not a perfectly homogenous group of Israelites.[6] While it's true that God called Israel to be set apart from the nations, their distinctiveness wasn't intended to foster self-righteous superiority. It was intended to make them a light to the nations, attracting them to the living God.

Peter wasn't the only one who missed God's plan. When Jesus reminded the members of Nazareth's synagogue that God showed grace to Gentiles in the time of Elijah and Elisha, they tried to throw him off a cliff.[7]

And let's not forget that the Gentiles were just as guilty as the Jews of racial prejudice. The emperor Claudius exiled Jews (including Jewish Christians) from Rome. When his reign ended and Jews slowly returned to Rome, the Gentile church didn't give them an enthusiastic reception. Instead, the Gentiles tried to assert their superiority.[8]

FOLLOWING JESUS SHOULD LEAD US TO FORM A WORLDWIDE TRIBE THAT WELCOMES EVERYONE AND CHARITABLY DIALOGUES OVER OUR DIFFERENCES.

No culture or century has escaped the effects of tribalism. In his farewell address, George Washington warned that political parties would tear the new nation apart.[9] Similarly, Mark Cuban, the billionaire owner of the Dallas Mavericks, told Bari Weiss that one of the greatest current dangers to our (now much older) nation is political parties. Cuban would love to see political parties abolished.[10] But the problem is that even if you dissolved all political parties today, new ones with all the same problems would form tomorrow.

So is there any way out of tribalism?

Join a Bigger Tribe

If we can't escape tribalism, then maybe we need to join a bigger tribe—a tribe into which everyone is invited.

But an inclusive tribe is counterintuitive.

By their very nature, tribes define who's in and who's out. The exclusiveness of tribes appeals to our sense of superiority. What a win for your tribe if Jesus is one of your members! Just think of all the moral and spiritual authority you accrue if you can claim Jesus is on your side of the white or black, Republican or Democrat, conservative or progressive tribe.

Of course, this wasn't always the case. Before Nathanael became one of Jesus's disciples, he demonstrated the human craving for tribalism by judging Jesus's hometown. When his brother Philip told him about Jesus, Nathanael scoffed. "Nazareth! Can anything good come from there?"[11] Nathanael grew up in Cana—he wasn't about to follow a rabbi from a backwater like Nazareth!

Whether it's political, cultural, racial, economic, or geographical, there's almost no limit to the ways tribes justify our moral superiority over others. "They" are from the wrong neighborhood. "They" have an inadequate education. "They" don't have the right views. "They" are never good enough, because most tribes demand you merit inclusion, and judge those who don't.

But Jesus is forming a worldwide tribe based on grace, not merit.

Because membership in Jesus's tribe can't be earned by good works or a good pedigree, there's no one to look down on. There's no moral superiority. There's no "us" vs. "them." In Jesus's tribe, everyone possesses dignity and value—even those who are currently outside of the tribe! Our king tells us to treat everyone with equality and respect.

Jesus is building a multi-national, multi-lingual, multi-ethnic community of followers. Dr. Dawson and I, along with *everyone* else who follows Jesus as Lord, are part of the *same* tribe.[12]

And if you aren't already a part of this tribe, you're welcome to join!

Discussion and Reflection Questions

1. The disciples found it hard to believe that Samaritans would be included in God's kingdom. Who do you find it hard to believe will be included in God's kingdom?

2. In what ways do you think you're superior to people in other tribes? How can you resist that sense of superiority?

3. Read Revelation 5:9. How does this challenge your concept of who is included in God's kingdom? What do you find most exciting about being a part of a tribe that spans time, ethnic boundaries, national boundaries, political affiliation, and language barriers?

Conclusion

HOPE FOR THE FUTURE

As you come to the end of this book, I hope you're experiencing three things:

1. Conviction

I am a recovering tribalist. I know what it's like to give my loyalty to the donkey or the elephant instead of the lamb. I know that having a "them" to hate is a heady experience—almost as heady as finding a candidate *you know* will change things for good. I know that few forms of self-righteousness transcend the satisfaction of *being right and knowing it*. I've felt all of these things. I know I'll be tempted by them in the future. And that's why I'm so grateful that God refuses to give me over to the sins of tribalism. His conviction is a continual gift.

Maybe, as you've read this book, you've felt that same conviction. If so, be thankful. God is at work in your heart. Confess your failures, accept his forgiveness, and ask for the spiritual power to change. He will provide.

That said, if you've finished this book in a state of anger without any sense of conviction, you may be in a dire situation. In our experience, the most tribalized people have the hardest time admitting it.

They're so *self-assured* in the rightness of their tribe that they cannot admit any fault. Spiritual blindness to tribalism is a curse, not a blessing. But we aren't condemning you. We're encouraging you: sit down with someone you trust—a spouse or friend or coworker— and ask if they see signs of tribalism in your life.

Tribalism wrecks lives, but Jesus heals. Embrace this good news and see what happens.

2. Understanding

Hopefully you see why tribalism is so attractive. You're wired for belonging, but this good desire goes bad when belonging to an "us" requires despising a "them." In the twenty-first century, new technology is accelerating tribalism by algorithmically imprisoning us in echo chambers where tribal truths reign over Universal Truth. Meanwhile, the places and institutions that once connected diverse people are shuttering their doors, making it ever easier to caricature the opponents you no longer know or understand. This unhealthy tribalism incentivizes inauthenticity, escalates cultural anxiety, obscures the truth, and does not tolerate diversity of thought.

> JESUS'S TRIBE—THE CHURCH—IS MULTI-LINGUAL, MULTI-ETHNIC, MULTI-NATIONAL, MULTI-PERSONALITY, MULTI-PERSPECTIVAL, AND MULTI-POLITICAL.

Yet there is such a thing as a healthy tribalism. A healthy tribe is one that welcomes *all* people and treats outsiders with kindness, generosity, and respect. Jesus's tribe—the church—is the only tribe open to everyone. It is multi-lingual, multi-ethnic, multi-national, multi-personality, multi-perspectival, and multi-political. By joining this tribe, you can enjoy a tribal sense of belonging without animosity toward outsiders. After all, Jesus's tribe exists, in part, to serve and love *them*.

3. Hope

When I began work on this book in April of 2020, I felt hopeless. Churches were warring over election results, masks, vaccines, critical race theory, LGBTQ+ inclusion, nationalism, QAnon, and more. They increasingly compromised the truth of the gospel to accommodate the tribal narratives of the right and the left.

Writing this book felt like a *necessary* plea. A last call to return to Jesus before the bar closed and the American church faded.

But there's still hope. Resisting unhealthy tribalism doesn't require an Ivy League degree. It requires a transformed heart. Jesus died to forgive your sins, and he rose again to make you new. You are part of a new humanity, formed in Jesus's image to reflect him to a lost and broken world.

Give him your allegiance and ask him to use your hands to rebuild what tribalism broke. The task might seem daunting, but don't lose hope. The king who sits on the throne of heaven empowers you to cross tribal boundaries, admit when you don't know, listen to others, show radical generosity, and give the gift of kindness to your enemies. These actions will always seem strange to tribalists—and to the part of your heart that wants to go back to unhealthy tribalism!—but nothing could be more ordinary to those following Jesus.

Jesus can transform me. Jesus can transform you. Jesus can transform us. That is why I am *no longer* hopeless. I hope you are not hopeless either.

You Aren't Alone

If you're anything like me, the culture wars have left you feeling politically homeless, theologically orphaned, and culturally alone. Trust me, you are *not* alone.

When Keith and I launched our podcast, *Truth Over Tribe*, we began to have conversations with pastors, leaders, and Christian thinkers all over the country. And we realized that we were not alone. There are faithful churches all over the country who put Jesus above partisan loyalties. The light of the church in America may be flickering, but it won't be extinguished. Although it's tempting, despair is not an option for followers of Jesus. How do you give up hope when you follow a resurrected king who established the church and promised the gates of hell would not overcome it?

God's spirit is actively renewing his people *around the world*. Christians are seeing the damage that political tribalism has done to Jesus's reputation. We're confessing the ways we put hope in politics over God. We're recanting our allegiance to the elephant and the donkey. We're repenting of how we compromised our prophetic witness for the sake of worldly power. And we're committing ourselves to the king and his kingdom's politic, rather than an earthly party's platform.

Tribalism may force the church through a painful realignment. But that won't be the last chapter. The seeds of renewal—confession, forgiveness, transformation, prayer—are already being sown.

If you share our vision for a non-tribal, non-politically compromised church, then know you aren't alone. If you want to help God build a church body characterized by God's politic and love of enemies, then know that you do not build alone. We're with you. Jesus is with you. His spirit is with you.

TRIBALISM MAY FORCE THE CHURCH THROUGH A PAINFUL REALIGNMENT. BUT THAT WON'T BE THE LAST CHAPTER.

Join us in praying that God would renew his people. Start a conversation in your church or in your community about unhealthy and healthy tribalism. Read a book together. Make a friendship across tribal lines. Offer radical generosity to someone in a different tribe. Show kindness to someone who hurts you.

But whatever you do, don't lose hope. Jesus is king. He has not left his throne. He will return. And until he does: worship him alone. The love of God is the only fire hot enough to melt the hatred of tribalism.

Discussion and Reflection Questions

1. What is one way this book has convicted you of tribalism that you don't want to forget going forward?

2. How has your understanding of tribalism changed or developed by reading this book?

3. How do you hope the church will change in the future to resolve the problems created by tribalism?

Notes

Chapter 1: Tribalism Ruins Your Relationships

1. Tovia Smith, "'Dude, I'm Done': When Politics Tears Families and Friendships Apart," *All Things Considered*, NPR, October 27, 2020, www.npr.org/2020/10/27/928209548/dude-i-m-done-when-politics-tears -families-and-friendships-apart.

2. Don't watch *The Simpsons?* See "Cheese-Eating Surrender Monkeys," TVTropes, accessed March 29, 2022, https://tvtropes.org/pmwiki/pmwiki.php /Main/CheeseEatingSurrenderMonkeys.

3. Liz Mineo, "Good Genes Are Nice, but Joy Is Better," *Harvard Gazette*, April 11, 2017, https://news.harvard.edu/gazette/story/2017/04/over-nearly-80-years -harvard-study-has-been-showing-how-to-live-a-healthy-and-happy-life/.

4. Judith Margolis Friedman, "This Is Social Suicide, but OK, Here Goes," *Times of Israel*, October 12, 2020, https://blogs.timesofisrael.com/a-social-suicide-note -of-sorts/.

5. "This Photo of Ellen and George W. Bush Will Give You Faith in America Again," YouTube, *Ellen Show*, October 7, 2019, www.youtube.com/watch ?v=lSZtjol7mJA.

Chapter 2: Tribalism Makes You Anxious

1. Ben Smith, "I'll Take 'White Supremacist Hand Gestures' for $1,000," *New York Times*, May 16, 2021, www.nytimes.com/2021/05/16/business/media /jeopardy-hand-gesture-maga-conspiracy.html.

2. Smith, "I'll Take."

3. Smith, "I'll Take."

4. Greg Lukianoff and Jonathan Haidt, *The Coddling of the American Mind: How Good Intentions and Bad Ideas Are Setting Up a Generation for Failure* (New York: Penguin, 2018), 54.

5. Matthew 25:23.

6. David French, "Don't Let Fear of 'Wokeness' Close Hearts and Minds," Dispatch, May 16, 2021, https://frenchpress.thedispatch.com/p/dont-let-fear -of-wokeness-close-hearts.

7. David French, "An Important Apology Shows the Path Past Christian Trumpism," Dispatch, January 24, 2021, https://frenchpress.thedispatch.com /p/an-important-apology-shows-the-path.

Chapter 3: Tribalism Incentivizes Inauthenticity

1. Bronnie Ware, *The Top Five Regrets of the Dying: A Life Transformed by the Dearly Departing* (Alexandria, NSW: Hay House Australia, 2019), 44.

2. Dorian Abbot, "MIT Abandons Its Mission. And Me," Common Sense, October 5, 2021, https://bariweiss.substack.com/p/mit-abandons-its-mission -and-me.

3. Abbot, "MIT Abandons Its Mission."

4. "J. K. Rowling Writes about Her Reasons for Speaking Out on Sex and Gender Issues," JKRowling.com, June 10, 2020, www.jkrowling.com/opinions /j-k-rowling-writes-about-her-reasons-for-speaking-out-on-sex-and-gender-issues/.

5. Michael Wines, "Florida Bars State Professors from Testifying in Voting Rights Case," *New York Times*, November 4, 2021, www.nytimes.com/2021 /10/29/us/florida-professors-voting-rights-lawsuit.html.

6. "A Letter on Justice and Open Debate," *Harper's Magazine*, July 7, 2020, https://harpers.org/a-letter-on-justice-and-open-debate/.

7. Jessica Wolf, "The Truth about Galileo and His Conflict with the Catholic Church," UCLA Newsroom, December 22, 2016, https://newsroom.ucla.edu /releases/the-truth-about-galileo-and-his-conflict-with-the-catholic-church.

8. Hans Christian Andersen, *The Emperor's New Clothes*, American Literature, accessed March 30, 2022, https://americanliterature.com/author/hans-christian -andersen/short-story/the-emperors-new-clothes.

Chapter 4: Tribalism Creates Your Enemies

1. Lilliana Mason, *Uncivil Agreement: How Politics Became Our Identity* (Chicago: University of Chicago Press, 2018), 50–52.

2. Mason, *Uncivil Agreement*, 50–52.

3. Mason, *Uncivil Agreement*, 1–23.

4. Mason, *Uncivil Agreement*, 43.

5. Mason, *Uncivil Agreement*, 10–11.

6. Mason, *Uncivil Agreement*, 11.

7. Mason, *Uncivil Agreement*, 11.

8. Greg Lukianoff and Jonathan Haidt, *The Coddling of the American Mind: How Good Intentions and Bad Ideas Are Setting Up a Generation for Failure* (New York: Penguin, 2018), 57.

9. Matthew 5:43–44 NLT.

10. Romans 5:10.

Chapter 5: Tribalism Blinds You

1. John Fea, *Believe Me: The Evangelical Road to Donald Trump* (Grand Rapids, MI: William B. Eerdmans, 2020), 56.

2. Gary Bauer, "Clinton Corrupts Our National Culture," *Human Events*, September 25, 1998.

3. Albert Mohler, "Resolution on Moral Character of Public Officials," Southern Baptist Convention, June 1, 1998, www.sbc.net/resource-library/resolutions /resolution-on-moral-character-of-public-officials/.

4. John Fea, "What James Dobson Said in 1998 about Moral Character and the Presidency," *Current*, June 25, 2016, https://currentpub.com/2016/06/25/james -dobson-on-the-character-of-the-president-of-the-united-states/.

5. Jonathan Allen and Jonathan Stempel, "FBI Documents Point to Trump Role in Hush Money for Porn Star Daniels," Reuters, July 18, 2019, www.reuters.com /article/us-usa-trump-cohen/fbi-documents-point-to-trump-role-in-hush-money -for-porn-star-daniels-idUSKCN1UD18D.

6. Sarah Eekhoff Zylstra, "Dobson Explains Why He Called Trump a 'Baby Christian,'" *Christianity Today*, August 4, 2016, www.christianitytoday.com /news/2016/august/james-dobson-explains-why-donald-trump-baby-christian

.html; and "James Dobson: Why I Am Voting for Donald Trump," *Christianity Today*, September 23, 2016, www.christianitytoday.com/ct/2016/october/james -dobson-why-i-am-voting-for-donald-trump.html.

7. Robert Jeffress, *Twilight's Last Gleaming: How America's Last Days Can Be Your Best Days* (Franklin, TN: Worthy, 2011), 103; and Michel Martin, "Pastor Robert Jeffress Explains His Support for Trump," NPR, October 16, 2016, www.npr.org/2016/10/16/498171498/pastor-robert-jeffress-explains-his-support-for-trump.

8. Martin, "Pastor Robert Jeffress."

9. Albert Mohler, "Christians, Conscience, and the Looming 2020 Election," AlbertMohler.com, October 26, 2020, https://albertmohler.com/2020/10/26 /christians-conscience-and-the-looming-2020-election.

10. Jonathan Haidt, *The Happiness Hypothesis: Putting Ancient Wisdom to the Test of Modern Science* (London: Cornerstone Digital, 2015), 8.

11. See Romans 1:28 and Ephesians 4:17.

12. Michael Specter, "Freedom from Fries: Can Fast Food Be Good for You?," *New Yorker*, October 26, 2015, www.newyorker.com/magazine/2015/11/02 /freedom-from-fries, emphasis added.

13. Jeremiah 17:9 ESV.

14. Adam Grant, *Think Again: The Power of Knowing What You Don't Know* (New York: Viking, 2021), 47.

15. Grant, *Think Again*, 15–33.

16. Grant, *Think Again*, 65.

17. Grant, *Think Again*, 70–71.

18. Justin Giboney, interviewed by Keith Simon, *Truth Over Tribe* (podcast), September 29, 2021.

19. Romans 1:23.

20. Romans 1:28–30.

21. Romans 3:21–26.

22. Romans 5:17.

Chapter 6: Why Your Brain Is Tribal

1. Jeff Ashby, quoted in Adam Grant, *Think Again: The Power of Knowing What You Don't Know* (New York: Viking, 2021), 129.

2. Pat Pickens, "Amazing Maps of the Sports World," Stadium Talk, August 13, 2020, www.stadiumtalk.com/s/sports-maps-a16f005a291342b6.

3. Grant, *Think Again*, 126–35.

4. Grant, *Think Again*, 125.

5. Carsten K. W. De Dreu et al, "Oxytocin Promotes Human Ethnocentrism," PNAS, January 10, 2011, www.pnas.org/doi/10.1073/pnas.1015316108.

6. Jonathan Haidt, *The Righteous Mind: Why Good People Are Divided by Politics and Religion* (Vancouver, BC: Langara College, 2020), 236.

7. John Mark Comer, interviewed by Patrick Miller, *Truth Over Tribe* (podcast), September 15, 2021.

Chapter 7: Why Your Facebook Feed Is Tribal

1. Joe Pinsker, "Trump's Presidency Is Over. So Are Many Relationships," *Atlantic*, March 30, 2021, www.theatlantic.com/family/archive/2021/03/trump-friend-family-relationship/618457/

2. Pinsker, "Trump's Presidency Is Over."

3. Jeff Horwitz and Deepa Seetharaman, "Facebook Executives Shut Down Efforts to Make the Site Less Divisive," *Wall Street Journal*, May 26, 2020, www.wsj.com/articles/facebook-knows-it-encourages-division-top-executives-nixed-solutions-11590507499.

4. Shoshana Zuboff, *The Age of Surveillance Capitalism: The Fight for a Human Future at the New Frontier of Power* (New York: Public Affairs, 2020), 63–97.

5. Zuboff, *Age of Surveillance*, 63–97.

6. Zuboff, *Age of Surveillance*, 128–74.

7. Horwitz and Seetharaman, "Facebook Executives."

8. See John 8:23; 18:36. Compare with Romans 12:1–2; 2 Corinthians 10:2; Ephesians 6:12; 1 John 4:3.

9. John 8:23.

Chapter 8: Why Your Personal Truth Is Tribal

1. Ronald G. Shafer, "The Thin-Skinned President Who Made It Illegal to Criticize His Office," *Washington Post*, September 8, 2018, www.washingtonpost.com/news/retropolis/wp/2018/09/08/the-thin-skinned-president-who-made-it-illegal-to-criticize-his-office/.

2. "First Words: Thomas Jefferson, March 4, 1801," University of Virginia Miller Center, accessed April 1, 2022, https://millercenter.org/issues-policy/governance/first-words-thomas-jefferson-march-4-1801.

3. Interestingly, Gutiérrez even extends her argument by arguing for mathematical forms that are not anthropocentric. She suggests that children learn math from *birdsongs*. Rochelle Gutiérrez, "Living Mathematx: Towards a Vision for the Future," University of Illinois at Urbana-Champaign, October 5, 2017, https://files.eric.ed.gov/fulltext/ED581384.pdf.

4. Deborah McPhail and Michael Orsini, "Fat Acceptance as Social Justice," *Canadian Medical Association Journal*, September 7, 2021, www.cmaj.ca/content/193/35/E1398.

5. Mark Sayers, interviewed by Morgan Lee, "Why Someone You Love Might Join QAnon," *Christianity Today Quick to Listen* (podcast), September 9, 2020, www.christianitytoday.com/ct/podcasts/quick-to-listen/qanon-evangelicals-global-conspiracy-theory.html.

6. Emily Belz, "Sign of the Times," *World*, August 19, 2020, https://wng.org/articles/sign-of-the-times-1617297218.

7. Belz, "Sign of the Times."

8. Greg Locke, interviewed by Patrick Miller, *Truth Over Tribe* (podcast), November 23, 2021.

9. See Mark 5:9; 9:22.

10. See John 16:13.

11. See Mark 9:20–22.

12. John 18:38.

13. John 8:32.

14. Colossians 2:8.

Chapter 9: Why Your Community Is Tribal

1. Timothy P. Carney, *Alienated America: Why Some Places Thrive While Others Collapse* (New York: Harper, 2020), 94.

2. Genesis 2:18.

3. Maria A. Villarroel and Emily P. Terlizzi, "Symptoms of Depression among Adults: United States, 2019," Centers for Disease Control and Prevention, September 2020, www.cdc.gov/nchs/products/databriefs/db379.htm.

4. Jillian McKoy, "Depression Rates in US Tripled When the Pandemic First Hit—Now, They're Even Worse," Boston University, October 7, 2021, www.bu.edu/articles/2021/depression-rates-tripled-when-pandemic-first-hit/.

5. David Brooks, "The Nuclear Family Was a Mistake," *Atlantic*, March 2020, www.theatlantic.com/magazine/archive/2020/03/the-nuclear-family-was -a-mistake/605536/.

6. Carney, *Alienated America*, 240–41.

7. Carney, *Alienated America*, 240–41.

8. Alexis de Tocqueville, *Democracy in America*, trans. Harvey C. Mansfield (Chicago: University of Chicago Press, 2002), 663.

9. See Revelation 7:9.

10. Romans 12:3, 5.

11. Romans 15:7 NLT.

Chapter 10: You Journey toward Eden

1. *Grand Canyon*, directed by Lawrence Kasdan (Century City, CA: Twentieth Century Fox, 1991).

2. Matthew Healy et al., "If I Believe You," track 6 on The 1975, *I Like It When You Sleep, for You Are So Beautiful yet So Unaware*, Dirty Hit, 2016.

3. Genesis 4:16.

4. Ben Wofford, "Up in the Air: Meet the Man Who Flies around the World for Free," *Rolling Stone*, July 20, 2015, www.rollingstone.com/feature/up-in-the -air-meet-the-man-who-flies-around-the-world-for-free-43961/.

5. Wofford, "Up in the Air."

6. C. S. Lewis, *The Weight of Glory and Other Addresses* (New York: HarperOne, 1980), 32.

Chapter 11: You Show Generosity and Kindness

1. Luke 4:17–21.

2. Ephesians 2:14–15.

3. 2 Corinthians 8:9.

4. "2019 Poverty Guidelines," Office of the Assistant Secretary for Planning and Evaluation, accessed April 2, 2022, https://aspe.hhs.gov/topics/poverty-economic -mobility/poverty-guidelines/prior-hhs-poverty-guidelines-federal-register -references/2019-poverty-guidelines.

5. Brad Edwards, *Everything Just Changed* (podcast), December 13, 2021.

6. James 2:16.

7. Philippians 4:8.

8. John 13:35.

9. Luke 23:34.

Chapter 12: You Pledge Allegiance to Jesus

1. Kate Shellnutt, "The UK's Highest-Ranking Evangelical Politician Steps Down," *Christianity Today*, June 14, 2017, www.christianitytoday.com /news/2017/june/uk-evangelical-tim-farron-steps-down-liberal-democrats.html.

2. Shellnutt, "UK's Highest-Ranking Evangelical."

3. See Matthew 4:23; 9:35; 24:14; Mark 1:15; Luke 4:43; 8:1; 16:16.

4. Lee C. Camp, *Scandalous Witness: A Little Political Manifesto for Christians* (Grand Rapids, MI: William. B. Eerdmans, 2020), 4.

5. Psalms 2:4; 103:19; 123:1.

6. Acts 7:55–56; Hebrews 1:3; Revelation 3:21.

7. Philippians 3:20; 1 Thessalonians 4:17.

8. Philippians 3:20.

9. John 3:16.

10. Matthew 19:28; Acts 3:21; 1 Corinthians 15:20.

11. See Mark 1:15. Compare with Isaiah 52:7.

12. Craig A. Evans, "Mark's Incipit and the Priene Calendar Inscription: From Jewish Gospel to Greco-Roman Gospel," Trinity Western University, accessed

April 3, 2022, https://web.archive.org/web/20170829065710/http://craigaevans
.com/Priene%20art.pdf, emphasis added.

13. Isaiah 52:7.

14. John 19:12, 15, 19 ESV.

15. Acts 2:25–31; 13:22–23.

16. Ephesians 2:8.

17. James 2:19.

18. "Naturalization Oath of Allegiance to the United States of America," US
Citizenship and Immigration Services, July 5, 2020, www.uscis.gov
/citizenship/learn-about-citizenship/the-naturalization-interview-and-test
/naturalization-oath-of-allegiance-to-the-united-states-of-america.

Chapter 13: You Admit When You Don't Know

1. Matthew 28:16–20 and John 10:16.

2. Acts 15 records the first church council, wherein the apostles debated about
whether Gentiles could be welcomed into their (at the time) mostly Jewish fel-
lowship. Part of the debate was practical: Did Gentiles need to be circumcised,
could they eat meat sacrifice to idols, could they continue in sexual immorality?
The church decided that the sexual immorality and sacrificial meat eating needed
to end, but also decided that they did not need to be circumcised (the primary
marker of a male's Jewish identity). This was how they fostered unity across
ethnic groups. Disunity wasn't an option.

3. Proverbs 19:2 NLT.

4. Psalm 49:13–14 ESV.

5. Brian Duignan, "Dunning-Kruger Effect," Encyclopedia Britannica,
September 8, 2020, www.britannica.com/science/Dunning-Kruger-effect.

6. Matthew 23:12 ESV.

7. Adam Grant, *Think Again: The Power of Knowing What You Don't Know* (New
York: Viking, 2021), 41.

8. Proverbs 12:15 ESV.

9. Romans 12:2 ESV.

10. Philip Yancey, interviewed by Keith Simon, *Ten Minute Bible Talks* (podcast),
November 18, 2021.

11. Mark 7:27–30 ESV.

12. Luke 2:40, 52.

13. See Proverbs 15:33.

14. Proverbs 15:33.

Chapter 14: You Cross Tribal Lines

1. "The Caning of Senator Charles Sumner," United States Senate, accessed April 3, 2022, www.senate.gov/artandhistory/history/minute/The_Caning_of _Senator_Charles_Sumner.htm.

2. "Stateside: A History of Mudslinging," Michigan Radio, November 6, 2012, www.michiganradio.org/politics-government/2012-11-06/stateside-a -history-of-mudslinging.

3. "Communism," The Martin Luther King, Jr., Research and Education Institute, August 4, 2020, https://kinginstitute.stanford.edu/encyclopedia /communism.

4. Luke 9:54.

5. Richard Brody, "What the Movies Miss about Trump's America," *New Yorker*, November 10, 2016, www.newyorker.com/culture/richard-brody/what-the -movies-miss-about-trumps-america.

6. Max Frankel, "President Won 49 States and 521 Electoral Votes," *New York Times*, November 9, 1972, www.nytimes.com/1972/11/09/archives/new-jersey -pages-president-won-49-states-and-521-electoral-votes.html.

7. Bill Bishop, "For Most Americans, the Local Presidential Vote Was a Landslide," *Daily Yonder*, December 16, 2020, https://dailyyonder.com/for -most-americans-the-local-presidential-vote-was-a-landslide/2020/12/17/.

8. Bill Bishop and Robert G. Cushing, *The Big Sort: Why the Clustering of Like-Minded America Is Tearing Us Apart* (Boston: Mariner Books, 2009).

9. David Wasserman, "To Beat Trump, Democrats May Need to Break Out of the 'Whole Foods' Bubble," *New York Times*, February 27, 2020, www.nytimes.com /interactive/2020/02/27/upshot/democrats-may-need-to-break-out-of-the-whole -foods-bubble.html.

10. Douglas J. Ahler and Gaurav Sood, "The Parties in Our Head: Misconceptions about Party Composition and Their Consequences," Gaurav Sood, August 15, 2017, http://gsood.com/research/papers/partisanComposition

.pdf; "Most Who Identify as Republicans and Democrats View Their Party Connection in Positive Terms; Partisan Leaners More Likely to Cite Negative Partisanship," Pew Research Center, October 4, 2017, www.pewresearch .org/politics/2017/10/05/8-partisan-animosity-personal-politics-views-of -trump/8_04/; and "The Perception Gap," More in Common, 2019, https://perceptiongap.us/.

11. Jeff Horwitz and Deepa Seetharaman, "Facebook Executives Shut Down Efforts to Make the Site Less Divisive," *Wall Street Journal*, May 26, 2020, www.wsj.com/articles/facebook-knows-it-encourages-division-top-executives -nixed-solutions-11590507499.

12. Cass Sunstein, *Echo Chambers: Bush v. Gore, Impeachment, and Beyond* (Princeton, NJ: Princeton University Press, 2001).

13. Virginia Heffernan, "What Can You Do about the Trumpites Next Door?," *Los Angeles Times*, February 5, 2021, www.latimes.com/opinion/story/2021 -02-05/trumpite-neighbor-unity-capitol-attack.

14. Heffernan, "What Can You Do."

Chapter 15: You Listen

1. Seneca, "Letter 50" in *Moral Letters to Lucilius* (AD 63). See Charles André, "Seneca and the First Description of Anton Syndrome," National Library of Medicine, December 2018, https://pubmed.ncbi.nlm.nih.gov/29979335/.

2. Adam Grant, *Think Again: The Power of Knowing What You Don't Know* (New York: Viking, 2021), 34.

3. Proverbs 15:32 ESV.

4. Proverbs 5:13–14 ESV.

5. Proverbs 25:12 ESV.

6. Proverbs 12:15 ESV.

7. 1 Kings 12:10–11 ESV.

8. Nicholas Kristof, "A Confession of Liberal Intolerance," *New York Times*, May 7, 2016, www.nytimes.com/2016/05/08/opinion/sunday/a-confession-of-liberal -intolerance.html.

9. Kristof, "Confession of Liberal Intolerance."

10. George A. Yancey, *Compromising Scholarship: Religious and Political Bias in American Higher Education* (Waco, TX: Baylor University Press, 2017), n.p.

11. Alison Reynolds and David Lewis, "Teams Solve Problems Faster When They're More Cognitively Diverse," *Harvard Business Review*, March 30, 2017, https://hbr.org/2017/03/teams-solve-problems-faster-when-theyre-more -cognitively-diverse.

12. Reynolds and Lewis, "Teams Solve Problems."

13. Proverbs 15:31–32 ESV.

14. Galatians 4:8.

15. Romans 1:19–20 ESV.

Chapter 16: You Join an Inclusive Tribe

1. Emma VanDelinder, "Racial Climate at MU: A Timeline of Incidents in Fall 2015," *Columbia Missourian*, November 6, 2015, www.columbiamissourian.com /news/higher_education/racial-climate-at-mu-a-timeline-of-incidents-in-fall-2015 /article_0c96f986-84c6-11e5-a38f-2bd0aab0bf74.html.

2. C. W. Dawson, "Another Christian Perspective on the Sermon about Gender," *Columbia Missourian*, October 18, 2019, www.columbiamissourian.com/opinion /local_columnists/c-w-dawson-another-christian-perspective-on-the-sermon -about-gender/article_f5cfa78c-f1ce-11e9-9f39-ab7ef33af72f.html.

3. Dawson, "Another Christian Perspective."

4. Dawson, "Another Christian Perspective."

5. Romans 9:17; Psalm 106:7–8.

6. Exodus 12:38 ESV.

7. Luke 4:28–30.

8. Romans 14–15.

9. George Washington, "Washington's Farewell Address 1796," Avalon Project at Yale Law School, accessed April 4, 2022, https://avalon.law.yale.edu/18th _century/washing.asp.

10. Mark Cuban, interviewed by Bari Weiss, *Honestly with Bari Weiss* (podcast), June 14, 2021.

11. John 1:46.

12. Galatians 3:28.

Your journey away from tribalism doesn't need to end here. Join the growing community of Christians who pledge allegiance to the lamb by subscribing to our weekly newsletter and podcast. We interview today's leading Christian thinkers, respond to challenging cultural topics, explore the latest news, and discuss tough political questions—all without picking a team.

Scan the QR code below to subscribe today.

TEN MINUTE BIBLE TALKS

Daily time in God's Word is the best way to stay sober in a culture drunk on tribalism. These (almost) daily podcast devotions from Keith, Patrick, and several friends will help you connect with Jesus in the time it takes to do a chore or get to work.

If you want a fresh way to engage God's Word, scan the QR code below and subscribe.